BASIC ESSENTIALS™
MAP & COMPASS

Help Us Keep This Guide Up to Date

Every effort has been made by the author and editors to make this guide as accurate and useful as possible. However, many things can change after a guide is published—new products and information become available, regulations change, techniques evolve, etc.

We would love to hear from you concerning your experiences with this guide and how you feel it could be improved and be kept up to date. While we may not be able to respond to all comments and suggestions, we'll take them to heart and we'll also make certain to share them with the author. Please send your comments and suggestions to the following address:

The Globe Pequot Press
Reader Response/Editorial Department
P.O. Box 833
Old Saybrook, CT 06475

Or you may e-mail us at:

editorial@globe-pequot.com

Thanks for your input, and happy travels!

BASIC ESSENTIALS™ SERIES

BASIC ✸ ESSENTIALS™
MAP & COMPASS

REVISED SECOND EDITION

CLIFF JACOBSON

ILLUSTRATIONS BY CLIFF MOEN

The Globe Pequot Press

Old Saybrook, Connecticut

Basic Essentials is a trademark of The Globe Pequot Press.

Cover photo: Images ©PhotoDisc, Inc.
Cover design by Lana Mullen
Text and layout design by Casey Shain
Photo credits: p. 26, Suunto KB-20, courtesy of Suunto; p. 27, the Silva Ranger, Model 515 CL, courtesy of Silva, Inc.; p. 28, Brunton Company Outback™, courtesy of the Brunton Company.

Library of Congress Cataloging-in-Publication Data is available.

ISBN 0-7627-0481-0

This text is printed on recycled paper
Printed and bound in Quebec, Canada
Revised Second Edition/First Printing

Contents

About this New Edition

When I wrote the first edition of *The Basic Essentials of Map and Compass* in 1988, I was certain it would never need updating. After all, maps and compasses—and the procedures for using them—have been standardized for decades.

Nonetheless, a few things have changed. Regrettably, U.S. government agencies have created some confusion regarding map ordering by changing bureau names and/or mailing addresses. For example, the National Ocean Survey is now called NOAA/NOS (National Oceanic and Atmospheric Administration/National Ocean Survey). Whew! The NCIC (National Cartographic Information Center) has become the ESIC (Earth Science Information Center). Four ESIC field offices further complicate matters. The Canadians, on the other hand, have artfully simplified procuring maps. All maps, photos, and related materials are available from a network of dealers, and you can use your telephone and VISA card!

New on the scene is GPS, or Global Positioning System. Twenty-four orbiting satellites continually transmit positioning information—latitude, longitude, elevation, and time—which may be accessed by an electronic receiver, called a GPS. All you have to do is push a button and wait a few minutes for the instrument to lock on to a satellite signal! The down side is that hand-held GPSs are battery powered, so satellite tracking time is limited to the relatively short life of the batteries. Besides, to fully comprehend global positioning, you must know how to read a map and compass. For these reasons, it is unlikely that GPS receivers will eliminate the need to know the procedures in this book. You'll find more on global positioning at the end of chapter 5.

Preface

In 1979 the Minnesota Department of Natural Resources asked me to develop a wilderness navigation curriculum for schools and nature centers. I proposed that the prospective materials differ from existing orienteering formats by emphasizing backcountry *navigation* rather than competitive orienteering. Although navigational procedures are the same regardless of where you use your compass, orienteers have some real advantages over those who travel the lakes and forests.

For example, the orienteering game relies on deadly accurate large-scale maps that have magnetic declination lines drawn in. Lucky is the wilderness traveler who has such a thoughtful picture to guide the way. More often than not, outdoors people must make do with dated topographic maps or state park guides. Sure, good maps are available for just about every place in North America, but for one reason or other, few people have them. Wilderness navigation then should include the way things are as well as how they ought to be.

As I worked on the project, I discovered that outdoor enthusiasts would rather *do* than read, that probing, complex, route-finding procedures served only to confuse, while over-simplifying processes gave false confidence. And that the interpretation of contour lines—an essential component of land navigation—could, after the presentation of a few simple rules, be mastered by beginners in a matter of minutes.

Ultimately I developed a simplified approach to route finding, the rudiments of which are incorporated into this book. My own experience suggests that everything you need to know about using a map and compass is contained in these pages. If you proceed step by step through the chapters, you'll have no trouble finding your way in the wilderness. That's a promise.

Equipment Needed

It's pointless to begin the study of wilderness route-finding without the two most important tools—a map and compass. So before you begin your study, please assemble the following materials.

1. An orienteering-style compass. No other type works as well. Indeed, you will be *severely* handicapped by any other instrument! You'll find a thorough discussion of compasses in chapter 3. Excellent orienteering compasses are available from these companies:

   Silva Division
   Johnson Camping, Inc.
   P.O. Box 966
   Binghamton, NY 13902
   (607) 779-2200

   Suunto U.S.A.
   Optimus, Inc.
   2151 Las Palmas Drive
   Carlsbad, CA 92009
   (619) 931-6788

   Brunton/Lakota, Inc.
   620 East Monroe Avenue
   Riverton, WY 82501
   (307) 856-6559

2. Space and cost considerations prevent us from including a colored topographic practice map. Instead, we've downsized selected portions of full-size maps, pinpointing the information you need to know. While this should pose no learning difficulty, you may get the big picture more quickly if you have on hand a genuine topographic map that contains all the pieces of the puzzle on a single page.

   Any topo map will do, though, and the larger the scale, the better. A 1:24,000 (about 2.5 inches to the mile) American map, or a 1:50,000 (1.25 inches equals one mile) Canadian map is ideal. Why not get a map of your favorite hunting, fishing, or hiking area? Chapter 1 tells you how to order maps.

3. An inexpensive plastic protractor is a must if you don't have an orienteering-style compass. Otherwise, it's surplus baggage.

Maps
Getting Started

S ome years ago, while on a canoe trip in the Boundary Waters
Canoe Area of Minnesota, I rounded a point and saw a young
couple sitting dolefully on a rock, staring intently at what
appeared to be a map. When they saw me, the pair stood up
and waved frantically in my direction. Curiously, I paddled over, only
to discover the two were hopelessly lost.

The man told me they'd left the lodge the day before and had set out
with a complement of backpacking gear to hike a portion of the
Kekakabic Trail—an old fire road that runs from Ely to Grand Marais.
The trail crosses a number of area lakes, hence our chance meeting.
But the trail is poorly marked, and it's not maintained. Numerous
animal trails and canoe portages intersect the route and confuse things
considerably. A good compass and topo map are essential tools for
navigating the "Kek."

The man poured coffee while the woman continued to study the
map. "I think we're here," she said, tapping her finger on what
appeared to be a small knoll near the water's edge. Eagerly, she
looked to me for reinforcement.

I squinted wonderingly at the impossibly small scale (1:500,000)
map. Even with my bifocals, I could tell nothing.

"Where'd you get this map?" I questioned.

"From our outfitter," came the reply.

"Hmmm . . ." I walked back to the canoe and got my 1:50,000 topo
map and spread it out on the lichen-splashed outcrop.

"I believe you're here," I said, pointing to a drumlin some distance
from the perceived location. "How can you guys find your way around
up here with a map like this?"

"We can't!" came the ready answer. "Our outfitter said this was all
we needed, that it'd work fine."

"Yeah," I replied.

Fortunately, I had three sets of maps in my party, so parting with one caused no inconvenience.

As the case illustrates, you can't do good work without the right tools. A good map is *everything*. A compass alone won't do. A compass is useful *only if* you know where it leads you. And for that you need a map.

Even a simple state park or road map is better than no map at all. Example: Assume you're lost in a heavily-wooded area. You have a compass but no map and no idea where you parked your car or "went in." Being lost comes as quite a surprise. After all, you hadn't planned on going in "that far."

Realistic problems? You bet! Ask any excited deer hunter. Think hard. How can you find your way out of the woods?

There is one way. It's called *luck*. Maybe if you go in a straight line (on any compass bearing) far enough, you'll hit a road. Maybe!

Now let's redo the problem with the aid of a highway map (figure 1-1). Only this time we can be more specific. You're cruising south on Highway 24 towards Leadville. You park somewhere along the roadway then strike off roughly northeast into the bush. You stuff map and compass deep into your pockets. Surely you won't need them. After all, you're going only "a short distance."

Several hours later, your enthusiasm dampens. Edged against a stand of impenetrable pines, miles of "nothing" stand between you and your car. Now what?

Your highway map shows that roads border the woods all around. Granted, there's not much detail, but it's enough. A rough southwest bearing will bring you back to Highway 24. From then on, it's simply a matter of asking directions.

As you can see, even a gas station highway map or state park guide will get you "out of the woods," if you have a compass and can use it for finding rough directions.

Beyond Planimetric Maps

The trouble with road maps (Figure 1-1) and state park guides is that they're *planimetric,* which means they show topography in a dead-flat perspective. Hills and valleys don't mean much when you're driving a car. But put on your hiking boots and the mood changes. For cross-country—indeed *any*—wilderness travel, you need a map that shows all the ups and downs plus major stoppers such as swamps and canyon walls. *Topographic* maps, as they are called, provide a three-dimensional perspective of the land.

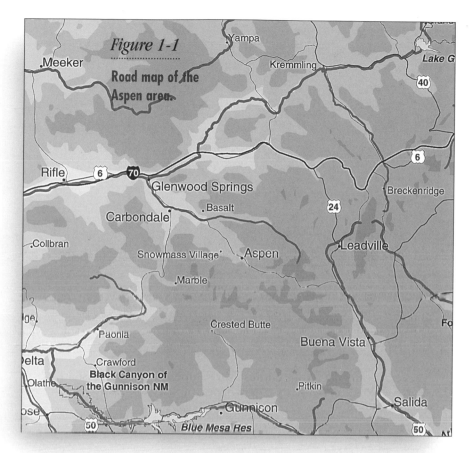

Figure 1-1
Road map of the Aspen area

Topographic Map Scales

All modern maps are made from aerial photographs that give a precise picture of the land. Cartographers (mapmakers) use these photos to construct topographic maps in a variety of scales, the most common of which are summarized below.

For American Maps

1:250,000 (1/250,000): One unit on the map equals 250,000 units on the ground. Each map covers one degree of latitude and two degrees of longitude (see discussion of latitude and longitude in the next section.) We Americans still work and think in the English system and our maps reflect our bias toward inches and feet. Here, 1 inch on the map equals 250,000 inches, or almost exactly 4 miles on the ground. As you might guess, one to a quarter-million maps don't show much detail.

1:62,500: Also called "15 minutes series," each map covers 15 minutes of latitude and 15 minutes of longitude. There are 63,360 inches to the mile, close enough so that 1 inch approximately equals 1 mile. This is probably the most useful and practical scale for backcountry use.

1:24,000 (7.5 minute series): 1 inch on the map equals 2,000 feet on the ground. Works out to a bit more than 2½ inches to the mile. These large-scale maps are great for precision navigation, but each one covers only about 55 square miles of territory, which means you'll need a lot of them if you're traveling very far. And at around three bucks per sheet, costs mount quickly.

For Canadian Maps

1:250,000 (same as American maps) and *1:50,000* are the most popular *traveling* maps in Canada. The 1:50s are particularly nice: Here, 1¼ inches equal one mile.

Colored or Monochrome?

Canadian maps in 1:50,000 scale are often available in monochrome (black and white) as well as colored editions. Consequently, forests (commonly shown as green areas) and lakes (colored blue) will appear in varying shades of gray.

Why get monochrome maps if colored ones are available? Two reasons: they cost less and photocopy better—important considerations if you need a lot of maps or duplications of certain sheets.

Unfortunately, American maps are not available in monochrome editions.

Land Use Information Series Maps

These are standard 1:250,000 Canadian topo maps that are over-printed with information about wildlife, vegetation, hunting and fishing, climate, and points of interest. They'll tell you where peregrine falcons nest, the migration routes and movements of caribou, the location of various fish species, and more. Land use maps tend to be pretty cluttered with data, so they're only marginally useful for navigation.

These maps are not available for all of Canada. Ask for the special Index to Land Use Information Series maps when you write the Canada Map Office.

Land Use and Land Cover Maps

These American maps are similar to Canadian Land Use Information maps, with these exceptions: *Land use* refers to how man's activities affect the land (for example, housing and industry).

Land cover describes the vegetation, water, and artificial constructions on the land surface. Scale is 1:100,000 or 1:250,000.

Where to Order Maps

Order American topographic maps from:

Branch of Distribution
U.S. Geological Survey
Box 25286, Federal Center
Denver, Colorado 80225

For charts and tide tables of U.S. coasts, the Great Lakes, sections of major rivers, and contoured fishing maps write:

National Oceanic and Atmospheric Administration/National Ocean
 Survey (NOAA/NOS)
Map & Chart Information, Distribution Branch N/CG33
Riverdale, Maryland 20737
(301) 436-6990

The Earth Science Information Center (ESIC) will help you find special-purpose maps and aerial photos (including space photos) of all kinds. It sorts and collects cartographic information from federal, state, and local government agencies. Write or call the ESIC office nearest you for a listing of city, county, and U.S. national park maps. National forest maps must be obtained from the U.S. Forest Service district office that manages the national forest of your interest. Your post office or public library can provide addresses. The ESIC will answer all your map questions and tell you what you need. They have a ton (well, at least five pounds!) of free pamphlets. You may phone for information, but you must order maps by mail.

ESIC Headquarters
Earth Science Information Center
U.S. Geological Survey
507 National Center
Reston, VA 22092
1-800-USA MAPS

Western Mapping Center, ESIC
U.S. Geological Survey
345 Middlefield Road
Melo Park, CA 94025
(415) 329-4309

Rocky Mountain Mapping Center, ESIC
U.S. Geological Survey, Box 25046
Denver, Federal Center, Mail Stop 504
Denver, Colorado 80225
(303) 236-5829

Midcontinental Mapping Center, ESIC
U.S. Geological Survey
1400 Independence Road
Rolla, MO 65401
(314) 341-0851

Until 1997, you could order Canadian topographic maps, Land Use Information Series maps, and aerial photos from the Canada Map Office. Now you have to buy them through a U.S. or Canadian map distributor. Write or call the Canada Map Office for a list of distributors. Canoeists should request the free pamphlet "Maps and Wilderness Canoeing."

Canada Map Office
Department of Energy, Mines, and Resources
615 Booth Street
Ottawa, Ontario Canada K1A 0E9
1-800-465-6277

For Canadian charts and tide tables:

Hydrographic Chart Distribution Office
Department of Fisheries and Oceans
1675 Russell Road, P.O. Box 8080
Ottawa, Ontario Canada K1G 3H6
(613) 988-4931, 32, 33
Fax (613) 998-1217

You can't order maps until you know what's in print. For this, you'll need an *Index to Topographic Maps,* available *free* from the agencies above. Write or call the USGS office in Denver or any ESIC office for American topographic map indexes. The Canada Map Office in Ottawa is your source for indexes to Canadian topographic maps and aerial photos. To get the right index, simply specify the state, province, or geographical region of interest.

When your index arrives, you're ready to order maps. Follow the detailed ordering instructions that come with each index, and you'll have no trouble finding the map you need in the scale you want.

Using Your Map

With your topo map in hand, you're ready to plan your route into the backcountry. Let's begin by identifying the important map features.

Map name: You'll find the map name in the upper and lower margins of American maps, and in the lower margin of Canadian maps. American maps also have names in parentheses that indicate adjacent quadrangles. For example, the map just southeast of ASPEN, COLO. (figure 1-2) is NEW YORK PEAK.

The Canadians use a slightly different system (figure 1-3). Here, the NAKINA name and location designation (42L) are included in a block diagram in the legend—a procedure that allows you to see the adjacent map sheets at a glance.

Scale: You'll find the representative fraction (1:24,000, etc.) and bar scale in the lower map margin.

Date: Most topo maps are very old; some were last field-checked in the 1950s. A lot has changed since then, especially the location of roads, dams, and other man-made features. The key words *revised* and *field-checked* will tell you when these maps were last updated.

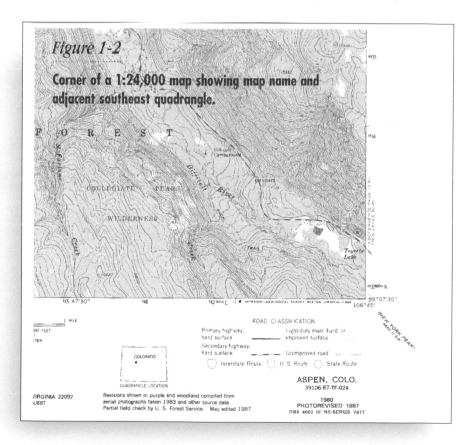

Figure 1-2

Corner of a 1:24,000 map showing map name and adjacent southeast quadrangle.

ASPEN, COLO.
39106-B7-TF-024

1960
PHOTOREVISED 1987
DMA 4662 III NE-SERIES V877

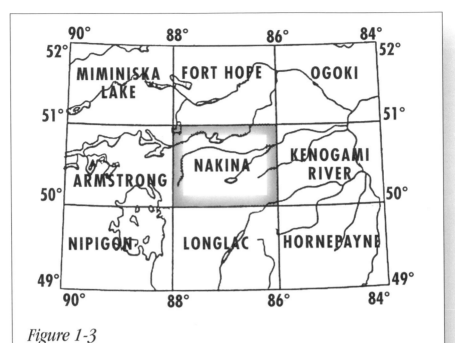

Figure 1-3

Index showing Nakina location and adjoining sheets on Canadian National Topographic System map.

Certainly, an old topo map is better than none at all. But it won't do if you're planning a remote hunting or fishing trip. If you need more current information than that supplied by your map, contact the government agency (U.S. Forest Service, Department of Natural Resources, etc.) nearest your area of concern. These professionals require current maps for their daily work. If they can't tell you where to get the maps you need, they'll help you update yours.

Latitude and Longitude: Your map is a bird's-eye view of a tiny portion of the earth's surface. But where does it fit onto the "big sphere"? By using *latitude* and *longitude* we can reference any location to a precise spot on the globe.

Lines of latitude (or parallels) run parallel to the equator, which is zero degrees. The *longitudinal* (north/south) lines that intersect at the poles are called *meridians,* or lines of longitude (figure 1-4). Longitude is measured in degrees east or west of the zero degree *prime meridian,* which originates in Greenwich, England.

BASIC ESSENTIALS

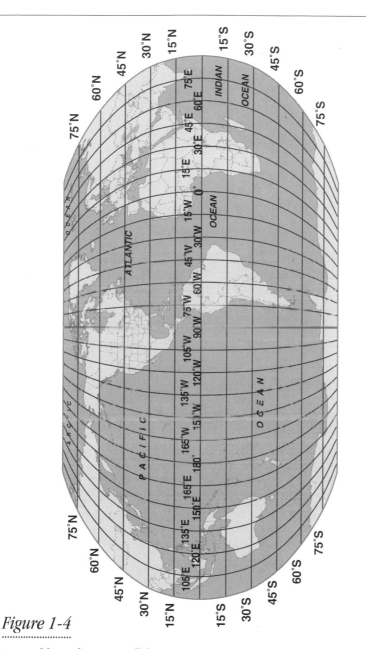

Figure 1-4

Lines of latitude run parallel to the equator. Lines of longitude run north–south and intersect at the poles.

By splitting latitude and longitude degree readings into smaller units, called *minutes* and *seconds,* specific points on the earth may be accurately located via a coordinate system. The rules are simple:

1° (degree) = 60' (minutes)
1' = 60" (seconds)

For example, Denver (see figure 1-5) is located at approximately 105° west longitude/39° 45' north latitude.

All this is needlessly academic, unless you plan to order specific large-scale maps and *aerial photographs.*

Aerial Photos

Suppose you're planning to canoe a remote river in Canada. Your topo map says you'll have to portage your gear around a major falls along the route. The map does not tell you where the portage begins, however. In fact, the *contour lines* (more on this later) suggest there's an impassable canyon wall on both sides of the river.

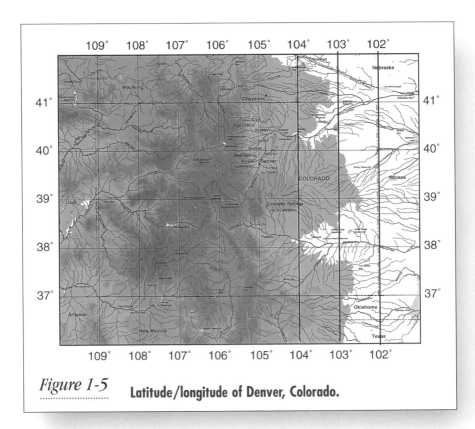

Figure 1-5 Latitude/longitude of Denver, Colorado.

Want to know more? Then order the aerial photographs from which your map was made. Photos will bring into clear perspective the most obscure features; more so if you specify *stereo pairs*. All you need is an inexpensive stereoscope (available at most hobby shops) to view the land in glorious 3-D. Now, you'll find a route around the falls ... if one exists!

Note: **Aerial photos are expensive, and they are very large scale (somewhere between 1:24,000 and 1:60,000.) Since there are *millions* of them on file, getting exactly what you want requires *precise* identification of the specific land feature to the nearest 5 minutes of arc.**

For those who don't understand the ways of latitude and longitude: Outline your area of interest on a topo map and send it along with your check to the ESIC or Canada map office. Your map will be returned with your order.

Which Way Is North?

"North," as everyone who has headed "up" north knows, is always at the top of the map. Well, sort of. And for conventional route-finding in the American Midwest, you can get by with that knowledge alone. However, if you plan to travel in the east or west, you'll need to take into account the differences between the *three* norths.

Most important is *true*, or geographical, north. That's the direction in which the lines of longitude run. Since the vertical lines that describe the right and left map margins are true meridians, any line on your map drawn parallel to them runs *true* north and south. Almost!

Meridians converge towards the poles, so the ones that run along your map edges *are not* truly parallel to one another (and the closer you get to each pole, the less parallel they become). No problem; that's what the "neat" lines are for.

Neat lines appear as tiny tick marks at equidistant points along all four map margins. To locate a true north–south meridian, simply connect the neat lines of equal value at the top and bottom of the map (figure 1-6 shows the relationship). Similarly, you can plot a true east–west line (parallel) by connecting the latitude neat lines. Then, you can use these coordinates to accurately plot the latitude and longitude of any point on your map.

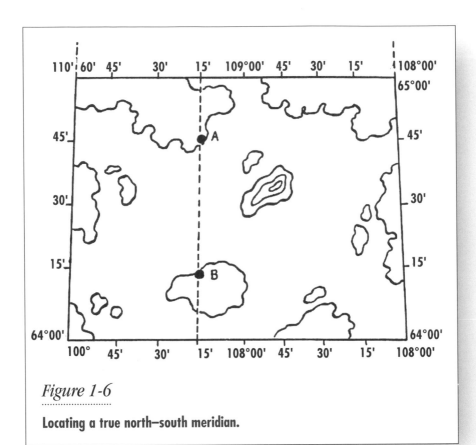

Figure 1-6

Locating a true north–south meridian.

The Other Norths

Grid north: All topographic maps have *grid lines* imprinted on their
faces. Grid lines began life as true meridians and parallels but
became distorted when the spherical earth was flattened onto
paper. Cartographers use a number of map *projections* to minimize
this distortion, but all are subject to some small error.
Consequently, grid lines usually *do not* point true north/south or
true east/west. The error is reported in a *declination* diagram
(refer to figure 4-8) in the bottom map margin, and is usually small
enough that it can be ignored by everyone but surveyors.

Grid north is the north you'll want to use when working with
civilian and military topographic maps. Use *true* north with maps that
don't have grid lines imprinted on their faces.

Magnetic north: Most everyone knows that the compass needle does not point to true north. Rather, it points toward the north magnetic pole that is located several hundred miles south of the real thing. The angular difference between the "three norths" is reported in declination diagrams or legend information on all topographic maps. In chapter 4 we'll have a lively discussion of how this affects navigation.

Contour Lines

The thin brown lines on topographic maps are called *contour lines.* They give "depth" and elevation to the land. You'll learn all about them in the next chapter.

Map Symbols

How do you tell (on a map) a school from a church? By the appropriate symbol, of course. There are dozens of map symbols, most of which are obvious. But lest you forget, Canadian maps emblazon them all in the margin or on the back. American USGS maps are more subtle. They tease you with a few road classifications, then assume you know the rest or have on hand their free pamphlet "Topographic Map Symbols," which lists them all.

How Brazen!

You'll find a listing of the most common symbols in appendix 1.

Tip: **It you have an old map, don't take the location of trails, unimproved roads, churches, and schools too seriously. It's quite possible that some of these man-made features no longer exist!**

You should also realize that, for clarity, map symbols *are not* drawn to scale—they always appear much larger than they really are. However, the *geometric center* of these symbols is accurately plotted. So shoot a compass bearing (or measure) there if you need to target a particular point.

Easy Map Reading

Understanding Map Contours

The light brown lines overprinted on topographic maps are called *contour lines*. They indicate the elevation above sea level (sometimes, other references are used) of land features and thus permit you to view the topography in three dimensions instead of two. Entire books have been written about contour lines and their interpretation; however, you'll get along quite nicely if you master these basics:

1. Contour lines connect points of *equal* elevation. Thus, closely spaced lines indicate lots of elevation change, whereas widely spaced lines show the opposite (figure 2-1). You gain or lose elevation only when you travel from one contour line to another. If you walk along a contour line, you'll be "on the level."

2. The *contour interval* (CI) is the vertical distance between contour lines. Its value in feet or meters is given in the lower map margin. Thus, if the CI is 50 feet, each successive contour line on the map increases or decreases (as the case may be) in elevation by exactly 50 feet. Each *fifth "index"* contour line is dark colored and is labeled with a number that gives its actual elevation above sea level.

3. The contour interval is determined by the cartographer, based on the amount of elevation change in the area. Mountainous regions will have a contour interval of 50 feet or more, while on relative flatlands it may be 10 feet or less. Consequently, the contour interval *is not* the same for all maps.

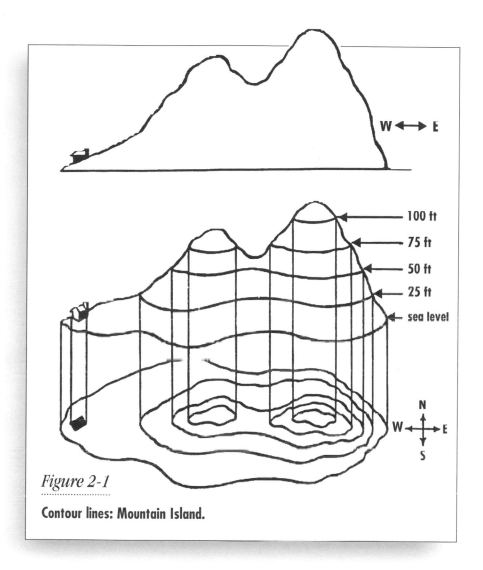

W ←→ E

100 ft
75 ft
50 ft
25 ft
sea level

N
W ←→ E
S

Figure 2-1

Contour lines: Mountain Island.

Tip: **Convert meters (foreign maps are all metric) to feet (1 meter equals 3.3 feet) if you don't think in the metric system.**

4. The larger the contour interval, the less clear are the characteristics of the area. In short, a map with a CI of 10 feet gives a clearer picture of the topography than one with a CI of 100 feet. Keep this fact uppermost in your mind when you plan a cross-country hiking or ski trip. Remember, the shortest distance between two points is a straight line only if you're not mountain climbing!

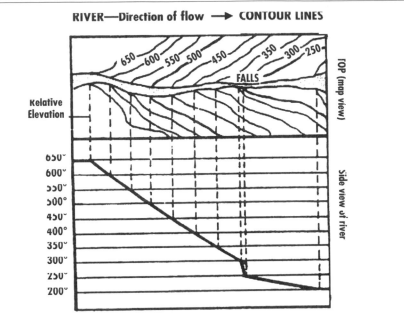

Figure 2-2

Falls are easy to spot on the contour map. Closely spaced vee points indicate a sudden drop. Notice the difference between the extreme elevation change at 300'–250' and the long decline between 250'–200'.

5. Where contour lines cross or run very close together, you'll find an abrupt drop—a falls or canyon (figure 2-2). Especially look for these closely spaced contour lines if you're boating an unknown river. If tight contours *intersect* your route, you can bet there are substantial rapids there.

To allay your concern, you may want to plot a river *profile* that shows the actual drop per mile.

Making the Profile

Begin by drawing a broad line along each side of the river, parallel to your route. These lines reference your route—and draw your eyes to the river—so you can quickly locate what lies ahead, without

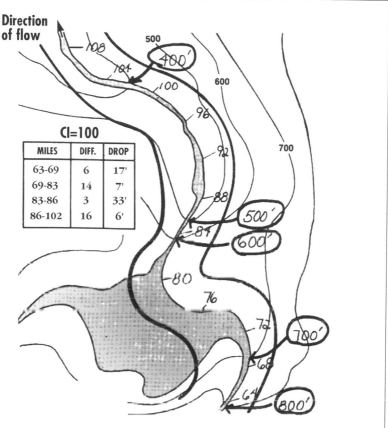

Direction of flow

MILES	DIFF.	DROP
63-69	6	17'
69-83	14	7'
83-86	3	33'
86-102	16	6'

CI=100

Figure 2-3

"The Map Profile" illustrates the techniques used to determine the drop of a typical river. Handwritten circled numbers indicate contours. Distances (miles) are not circled.

visual interference from other map features. I use a translucent felt-tip highlighter pen, the kind college kids prefer for marking important passages in textbooks.

Next, consult the map scale and mark the miles along your route. Gear the number of markers to the map scale. For example, on 1:250,000 maps, I label every 4 miles (figure 2-3), which works out to a mark every inch. On larger-scale maps I tick off each mile. The idea is to clarify without cluttering.

Now, get your pencil and draw a small arrow everywhere a contour line crosses the river. Write in the elevations of each contour near the penciled arrow and circle it. Be sure you indicate whether the elevation is in feet or meters.

You're now ready to compute the *drop*. Do the computations in a table similar to that in figure 2-3. For example, the 800-foot contour crosses the river at mile 63, while the 700-foot line intersects at mile 69. This is recorded in the table as *63–69*. The mileage difference is six (69–63). Dividing six into 100 (the value of the contour interval) yields a drop of 17 feet per mile.

From mile 69 to 83 the river drops less—7 feet per mile, etc.

In deciding if it's safe to boat an unknown river, keep these rules of thumb in mind:

a. A drop of 3 to 5 feet per mile is nice cruising for an open canoe or fishing boat. 10 feet per mile means gentle rapids. 20 or more is about the limit of an open canoe, and 35 may mean you'll have to portage your rubber raft. *Caution:* These are only guidelines! Maps tell you what to expect—not *what is!* Use your eyes to account for that!

b. Equally important as "drop per mile" is how the drops occur—whether uniformly, or at a falls, dam, or major rapid. Closely spaced drops mean a probable portage at those spots, though the rest of the river may be "user friendly." Uniform drops suggest a wild, fast ride, and your skills had best be up to it!

Note: **You can convert the "top view" of your profile to a side view for greater clarity. Figure 2-2 shows the procedure. You can also use this same method to draw a profile for land masses. Suppose you want to hike cross-country, but a large hill stands in the way. Can you walk the hill, or will you have to crawl up it? To find out the answer, simply draw a line from your location to your destination, and graph the drop as shown in figure 2-2.**

6. The closed or *vee* end of a contour line always points upstream (figures 2-2, 2-4). Note that this rule also applies to creeks, intermittent streams, and gullies.

7. Contour lines become U-shaped (the closed ends of the U's point *downhill)* to indicate the outjutting spur (ridge) of a hill.

8. The actual heights of many objects are given on topographic maps. For example, suppose you find the number 636X printed at a road

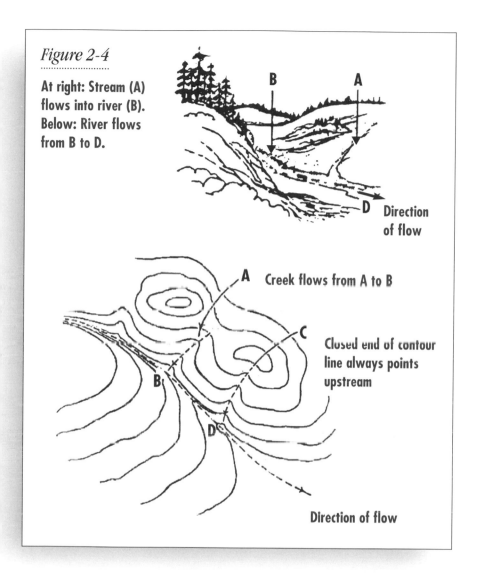

Figure 2-4

At right: Stream (A) flows into river (B). Below: River flows from B to D.

B   A

D   Direction of flow

Creek flows from A to B

Closed end of contour line always points upstream

Direction of flow

junction. This means that the X-marked spot is exactly 636 feet above sea level.

Contour Quiz

Use figure 2-5 to test your knowledge of contour lines. Answers are on the next page.

1. Is the creek flowing *into* or *out* of Pikitigushi Lake?

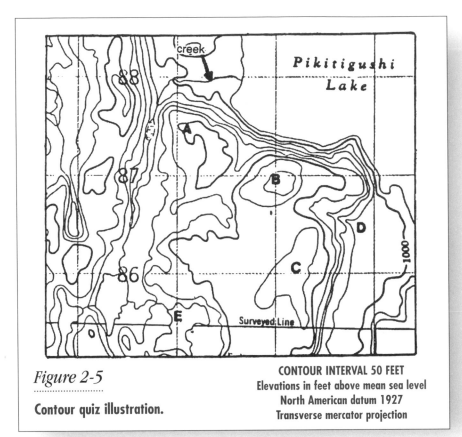

Figure 2-5

Contour quiz illustration.

CONTOUR INTERVAL 50 FEET
Elevations in feet above mean sea level
North American datum 1927
Transverse mercator projection

2. You are standing at point (a). What is your height above sea level? (Clue: notice the 1,000-foot contour to the east.)

3. You are standing at point (b), looking towards Pikitigushi Lake. Describe the topography directly in front of you.

4. You are walking south, from (b) to (c). Are you: a) gaining elevation? b) losing elevation? c) remaining level?

5. You walk from (b) to (d). Are you: a) going up a steep hill? b) going down a gully? c) going up a gully?

6. A creek joins lake (e) from the west. Does that creek flow *into* or *out of* lake (e)?

Answers to Contour Quiz

1. Into the lake. Remember, the closed ends of a contour line point *upstream.*

2. 1,250 feet. The index contour to the east is labeled 1,000. The contour interval is 50 feet; 50 feet x 5 lines = 250 feet of rise.

3. Very steep drop, almost a cliff. You wouldn't want to climb it.

4. You lose 50 feet of elevation (you go down 100 feet to the plateau, then climb 50 feet to reach [c]).

5. (b) Down a gully.

6. The creek flows *to the west,* out of lake "e."

Using the Bar Scale to Measure Horizontal Distances

Most of the time, maintaining map-ground scale relationships is simply a matter of remembering how many inches per mile the scale portrays, and interpolating accordingly. However, sometimes you want a more precise answer than your guesstimate provides. One way is to use the *bar scale* in the map legend, and a piece of scratch paper.

To compute the distance from (a) to (b) in figure 2-6, place the

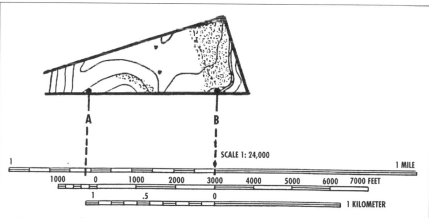

SCALE 1: 24,000

1 MILE

1000 0 1000 2000 3000 4000 5000 6000 7000 FEET

1 .5 0 1 KILOMETER

Figure 2-6

Mark the location of (a) and (b) on your paper, then compare it to the map bar scale.

paper edge between the points and transfer this distance to the scale below. You'll get a bit less than three-fourths of a mile.

You can also measure the distance directly with the graduated base-plate of your orienteering compass.

Preparing Your Maps for Use in the Backcountry

Maps are a joy to use if they're well organized and protected from the weather. Here are the recommended procedures:

1. Begin by outlining your route with a felt-tip highlighter. This way you can see where you're going at a glance.

2. If you're hiking or boating on a river or lake, you'll want to "tick off" the miles, as explained on pages 16–18, "Making the Profile." This will keep you from biting off more than you can swallow when you do your winter planning. Canoeists, kayakers, and rafters should carefully designate the location of stoppers such as falls and dangerous rapids and the positioning of portage trails. To allay your concern, you may want to draw a river (or trail) profile that shows the actual drop per mile.

3. Maps that will be frequently used in fishing boats are best glued to a thin plywood board, then clear-lacquered to protect them from water. Drill a hole in one corner of the board and attach a nylon security cord. You may also want to tie your compass to the board. Now, everything is at hand and protected from the elements.

Here are some other ways to waterproof your maps:

1. Insert them in Ziploc plastic bags. Giant 12½" x 16" Ziploc bags are available from office supply stores. Camping equipment shops (and most Boy Scout supply centers) carry heavier, similar-sized plastic envelopes with genuine zippers. If you want an inexpensive giant-sized map case, check out your local bait shop. Four-mil-thick "minnow" bags measure 32 x 17½ inches (these are also great for sleeping bags and clothing). Seal the mouth of each bag with duct tape.

2. Cover maps with clear contact paper—it makes them waterproof, but you can't write on them.

3 Paint on Stormproof—a clear chemical that's formulated for use on maps and charts. Most camping shops have it.

4. Apply Thompson's Water Seal—an industrial-strength chemical that's used for sealing concrete blocks. TWS is available in hardware stores in aerosol cans and tins. Apply it with a foam varnish brush. TWS (and Stormproof) makes maps water-repellent, not waterproof. You can write over it with pen or pencil.

5. No sense carrying map portions that you won't use. So trim away unnecessary paper with a scissors before you leave home. If you have a number of map sheets, use either of these methods for organizing them:

a. Glue the quadrangles together with rubber cement, accurately matching the latitude/longitude neat lines. Cut out important legend information and glue it to the map back or over a nonessential area.

b. Number individual map sheets consecutively. This works fine, except when you find yourself at the edge of a map sheet.

Maps that will be used in the field are better folded than rolled.

Tip: **Discover Forestry Suppliers, Inc., 205 West Rankin Street, Box 8397, Jackson, Mississippi 39204. This company carries a complete line of tools for the professional forester and geologist, including dozens of map aids and laminating films for maps and journals. They carry the complete line of Silva, Suunto, and Brunton compasses. Write for their catalog.**

Anatomy of the Compass

History

No one is certain where or how the compass originated, though it appears that the Chinese were first to discover magnetism in lodestone and its attractive power. One of the first working models consisted of a piece of lodestone floating on a cork in a bowl of water. Other primitive compasses, with magnets shaped like fish or turtles, can be seen in Chinese books that date to the eleventh and twelfth centuries.

The first clear description of a magnetic-needle compass is by Shen Kua, a Chinese, in A.D. 1088—about a century before the earliest mention in European texts. From then on, there are numerous references to compasses in Chinese literature as well as stories about their use by sailors "in dark weather or when the sky is overcast." Other references suggest that primitive compasses were used by Arabian merchants in A.D. 1200 and by Vikings a half century later.

It is not clear whether magnetism and its use for navigation was discovered independently in Europe or brought by travelers from China.

For a while the Chinese led the world in compass production, evidently because the hardened steel needed to hold the magnetism was not available in other parts of the world. But around 1400–1500, Europeans got into the act, and marine compasses became widely available. However, it wasn't until someone realized that compasses could be modified into sundials—and thereby substitute for the expensive watches of the day—that portable field compasses were born.

Little change took place until the end of the pocket sundial period, around 1750. Then came the development of sighting devices and the refinement of the "watch" or "box" compass, which survives today with few modifications.

In the twentieth century we saw substantial improvements in field compasses in the form of the Bezard compass of 1902 and the liquid-filled British Army compass of World War I. But it was not until the 1930s that the real excitement began. First came the development of reasonably-priced, liquid-filled orienteering compasses and birth of the Silva company, then the introduction of protractor-combined plate compasses and sophisticated sighting devices. Things continue on the upswing: The best of today's compasses are a tribute to engineering genius—a quiet lesson in sophisticated simplicity. (I am indebted to Björn Kjellstrom, inventor of the Silva compass, for this historical information.)

Modern Compasses

A half century ago route-finding was a precarious business. Maps of wilderness areas were not always accurate, and compasses were heavy, slow to use, not waterproof, and had no provision for computing bearings from a map.

Now all that has changed. The best modern compasses incorporate complete navigational systems. No longer do you have to grope for a pencil and protractor and "orient the map to north" to take a bearing. And don't let the plastic toylike construction of these instruments fool you. Most of the mid-priced ($15–$25) models can be *consistently* read to within 2 degrees of an optical transit—hand held! Even the cheapies seldom vary by more than 4 degrees.

There are four types of compasses: 1) *fixed-dial* or *standard needle* compass, 2) *floating dial,* 3) *cruiser,* 4) *orienteering*. For hiking, canoeing, hunting, fishing, and just about everything else, only the orienteering type (and where extreme accuracy is required, the floating dial with optical sights) makes much sense. Here are the differences:

Fixed-Dial Compass

Best typified by twenty-five-cent gumball machine models, these "questionably superior" versions of the old "box" compass have degree readings embossed on a fixed outer ring (figure 3-1). The needle rides on a hardened steel or mineral bearing in the center of the capsule. Fixed-dial compasses are slow to use, inaccurate, and not very versatile. People

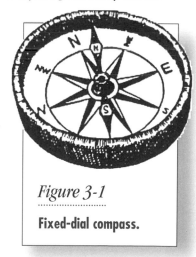

Figure 3-1

Fixed-dial compass.

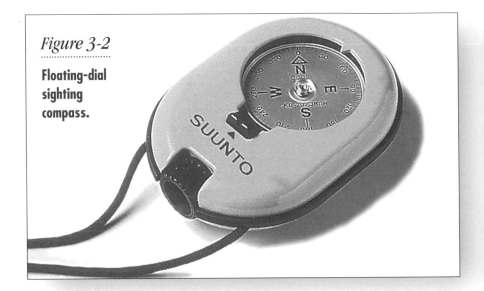

Figure 3-2

Floating-dial sighting compass.

buy them because they don't know how to use any other kind. About all these are good for is zipper pulls on jackets. Nonetheless, because they are so popular, you should know how to use then *effectively.* You'll find the specifics on page 34.

Floating-Dial Compass

The needle is an integral part of the numbered dial and spins freely on the pivot. You point the compass towards your objective and read the bearing at an index. There's nothing to set, usually, not even a cover to raise. Floating dial compasses run the gauntlet of quality— from five-dollar "hunter pin-on's" to sophisticated direct sighting models like the Suunto KB-14 or the KB-20 (figure 3-2) that can be interpolated to more than 15 minutes of arc.

Cruiser Compasses

These are professional-grade instruments that come in solid metal cases with protective hinged covers, onto which a "lubber's" (sighting) line has been inscribed. Numbers on the dial run counterclockwise (opposite to that of a fixed dial compass) so you can face your objective and the instrument where the north end of the magnetic needle intersects the dial.

Despite their dated design, "cruisers" are still widely used by foresters and geologists. They are accurate, heavy, slow to use, not waterproof, and very expensive.

Figure 3-3
....

A professional orienteering compass.

Orienteering Compasses—The Choice of Serious Outdoorspeople

Accuracy is only half the game. The other part is determining what numerical value to set on the compass. For this, you need a map and protractor.

Enter the *orienteering* compass (see figure 3-3). In 1933 Gunnar Tillander, an unemployed instrument worker, approached Björn Kjellstrom and his brothers Alvar and Arvid with a unique plan: Why not incorporate a protractor into the design of a standard needle compass? Almost overnight, the orienteering compass was born. It is unique for these reasons.

1. You can determine bearings from a map *without* the aid of a protractor and without orienting the map to north. This means you can make the computation from the seat of a bobbing canoe or while shuffling down a wilderness trail. You can even do it with mittens on!

2. Your direction-of-travel (bearing) is "locked" onto the compass dial. There's nothing to remember or write down. In fact, you don't even have to read the dial at all!

3. All orienteering compasses have ruled scales along their plastic base plates that make it easy to determine scale distances from a map.

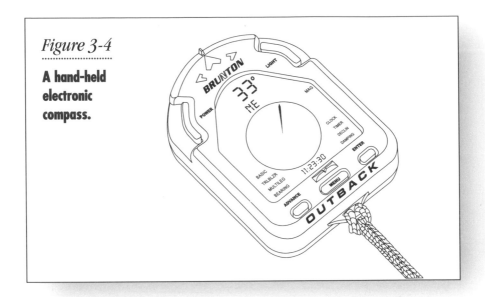

Figure 3-4

A hand-held electronic compass.

4. Orienteering compasses all have liquid-damped needles. Needle oscillation ceases in three to five seconds. The system works in temperatures down to 40 below zero.

5. The instrument is so simple that an eight-year-old can learn to run one in a matter of minutes.

For backcountry use, the orienteering compass has no peer. Unless you're running survey lines in search of buried treasure—in which case, you'll want an optical sighting compass—I can think of no reason why you should choose any other kind.

Because the orienteering compass is so versatile, the instruction in this book is centered around its use.

Electronic Digital Compasses

Technology has brought about a number of electronic compasses (see figure 3-4). Some have a memory and chronograph, plus an automatic shut-off switch to save battery drain. A few digital watches feature miniature electronic compasses, though none are accurate or versatile enough for serious navigation.

The best digital compasses are as accurate as the best needle compasses, and their bearings are much easier to read. The bad part is that electronic compasses are powered by batteries, which can fail, and they don't have built-in protractors to obtain map bearings and distances. This rules them out for backcountry use.

Accuracy: How Much Do You Need?

Surveyors and foresters need compasses that give readings to a fraction of a degree. But for general outdoor use, any instrument that will consistently read within 4 degrees of a transit will do, even for serious expeditions. You don't need 30-minute accuracy for navigating the backcountry. What you do need is a good map and *versatile* compass.

Consider this: One degree of compass error equals 92 feet per mile (tan 1° x 5,280) of ground error. A 4-degree error over a mile course will cause you to miss your objective by 368 feet—hardly significant when you consider *how* compasses are actually used. For example, rather than risk missing their objective (even by 368 feet), experienced travelers "aim-off." That is, they make a purposeful error to the left or right of the reference point. Then, they follow a road, trail, shoreline, powerline, or other "handrail" to their destination. Figure 4-5 in the next chapter details the procedure.

"Aiming-off" becomes even more important when you realize that man-made features such as buildings and trails are frequently misplotted on maps. Under these conditions, clear thinking is more important than precise headings. Here's what you need most in a "working" compass:

1. *Versatility* in transferring bearings from map to ground—hence, the desirability of the orienteering compass.

2. *Speed of operation:* Often, you need to determine a direction from the seat of a bobbing canoe or fishing boat.

3. *Carry ability:* Consider your compass an article of clothing, one you'll wear all the time. The lighter and more compact the instrument, the more pleasurable it will be to carry. Particularly, shun the compass with sharp, square edges. "Square corners" may be great for map plotting, but they'll eat through your clothes in a matter of minutes.

4. *Durability:* I once had a jeep run over an old Silva Ranger. The cover was smashed, but the instrument worked fine. That's tough! A field compass must be built to take everything from a bad fall to a thorough dousing.

5. *Amenities:* Are the scales on the base plate compatible with those on your map? Can the compass be compensated for area magnetic declination? (see chapter 4 for details). Night sights—either luminous or (better) a lithium light—are essential for black night travel. And if you're over age forty, a built-in magnifying glass will clarify map subtleties.

Damping

A compass needle will continue to oscillate for some time unless it is *damped,* either by a light-viscosity liquid *(liquid damping)* or by magnetism *(induction damping)*. Liquid-damped needles stop moving in about three seconds; induction-damped needles take much longer. As to longevity, the vote goes to induction damping, as there's never a chance for a leaky capsule.

However, induction-damped instruments are usually heavier, bulkier, and more expensive than liquid-damped ones. Nearly all the best hand compasses are currently liquid-filled. Except for the Brunton Pocket Transit professional model, induction damping has all but disappeared from the compass scene.

Sights

Some compasses come equipped with sights, which may or may not be a good thing. *Optical* (lensatic and prismatic) sights are most accurate and, in compasses of good quality, give results comparable to expensive surveying instruments.

When you look through an optical sight, you see image, graduated dial, and a vertical intersect line, all in the same plane. The result—in a well-built compass—is accuracy to a fraction of a degree.

Lensatic sights, like those on the old military field compass, are good or bad, depending on the precision of the sight assembly. The original U.S. Army lensatics could be read to 2 degrees of perfection or better. But the ten-dollar foreign copies that currently flood the market are another matter. Most won't read within 5 degrees of a transit!

Combination mirror-vee sight: There's a pop-up mirror with a vertical line scribed through its center. You adjust the mirror to a 60-degree angle (so you can see the alignment of the needle in the capsule), turn your body (not the compass) until the needle is centered within a printed arrow on the dial, then peer across the gunsight vee on the cover top towards your objective. Sounds accurate, and it can be, if you're extremely meticulous. Fact is, you can do as well—often better—by simply holding the instrument waist high and looking straight ahead. Accuracy of the system depends in large measure on precision mounting of the mirror and your ability to keep everything in alignment while holding it all rock-steady.

The problem with *all* nonoptical sights is their very short sighting plane—akin to shooting accurately a pistol with a 2-inch barrel. As explained, the accuracy of any sight depends on the precision and ruggedness of the mounting system. Unfortunately, most hinged compass sights lack the durability for long-term precise alignment. For this reason, your best bet is to use the "waist-high" method of sighting that is explained at the end of this chapter.

Here's what you can expect from the various styles:

Compass Type	Probable Maximum Error Without Practice	Probable Maximum Error With Considerable Practice	Approximate Time to Take An Accurate Bearing
Optical sighting	1 degree	½ degree or less	15 seconds
Orienteering	4 degrees	1½ degrees	10 seconds
Induction-damped cruiser	4 degrees	1½ degrees	20 seconds
Liquid-damped fixed-dial	10 degrees	5 degrees	15 seconds

Figure 3-5

Characteristics of various compass styles.

Declination

Some compasses have a mechanical adjustment for magnetic declination. This feature is quite inexpensive and is necessary only if you live in an area where declination values are large, or if you are confused by the mathematics of its computation. See the next chapter for details.

Inclination

The earth behaves like a giant magnet, and the closer you get to the poles, the greater the magnetic force. This causes the north end of the needle to tip down in the Northern Hemisphere and to rise in the Southern Hemisphere. Consequently, the compass needle must be balanced for the zone of operation so the needle will spin freely on its pivot.

Professional surveying instruments have a movable counterweight on the needle tail, which can be repositioned if necessary. Field compasses, however, come from the factory balanced for the zone of use. Most any compass you buy in the United States will work fine in North America. Hiking in Ecuador is another matter! Instruments that are balanced for far northern and southern zones are available on special order from the best compass makers.

Dial Graduations

The best compasses have dials that are graduated in 1- or 2-degree increments. Having more graduations than this simply clutters the dial. However, a lot of fine instruments have 5-degree graduations (especially those with small dials), and this is quite suitable for a field compass.

The rule is that you can interpolate a bearing by twice splitting the distance between the graduations on either side of the index. Thus, a 2-degree dial can be guesstimated to ½ degree; a 5-degree dial to 1¼ degrees, etc. So if you need the most precise readings, opt for finer graduations.

It's important to realize that precision bearings are only useful when combined with optical sighting systems. They are of little value in an orienteering compass. That's because orienteering instruments are almost never "read." Instead, the needle is aligned in the "doghouse" (printed arrow inside the capsule) and the direction-of-travel arrow on the base plate is followed. There is no need to read specific numbers. Indeed, orienteering compasses need not be graduated at all!

How Much Does a Good Compass Cost?

At this writing, twenty bucks will buy all the compass you need for wilderness travel. Paying more won't necessarily buy more accuracy or versatility. Options such as declination adjustments, night sights, and sighting devices drive up costs and add little utility. Fact is, the least expensive orienteering models are suitable for the most complex lake and land navigation you're likely to encounter. You *don't* need a professional compass for touring the backcountry.

How to Use the Waist-High Method of Sighting Your Orienteering Compass

Here's the most accurate way to take a bearing to a distant object with an orienteering compass:

Cradle the compass in your right hand and frame the dial with the thumb and forefinger of your left hand (figure 3-6). Forearms should be held gently but firmly against the body to provide a three-point (triangular) position, the apex of which is the compass.

Locate the compass *directly* along the midline of your body, just above your waist and a comfortable distance (about 6 inches) away from your stomach.

Next, turn your body (*not the compass*) until the direction-of-travel arrow on the compass base plate is pointing towards the objective whose bearing you want to determine. Then, while holding the base

Read Compass at Index Described on Dial

Figure 3-6

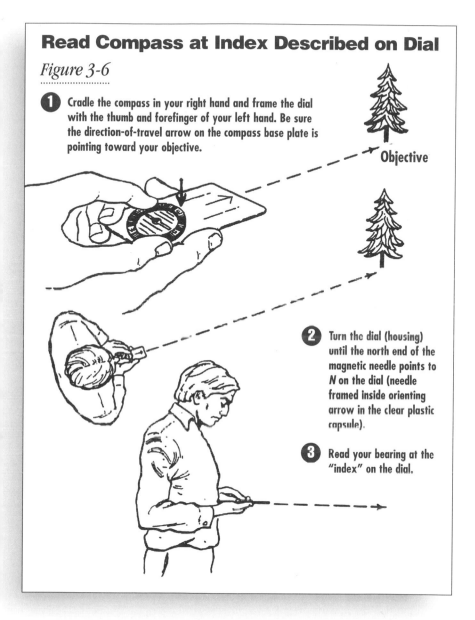

1 Cradle the compass in your right hand and frame the dial with the thumb and forefinger of your left hand. Be sure the direction-of-travel arrow on the compass base plate is pointing toward your objective.

Objective

2 Turn the dial (housing) until the north end of the magnetic needle points to *N* on the dial (needle framed inside orienting arrow in the clear plastic capsule).

3 Read your bearing at the "index" on the dial.

plate steady, turn the compass housing until the magnetic needle is framed inside the orienting arrow "doghouse" in the clear plastic capsule.

Now, take three "eye-shift" readings to your objective; that is, sight three times from the compass housing to the objective, *without* moving your head. When the alignment of everything—needle in doghouse, direction-of-travel arrow, and objective—is perfect, read your bearing. It should be within 2 degrees of an optical transit.

How to Take an Accurate Bearing with a Fixed-Dial Compass

Although experienced wilderness travelers rely entirely on orienteering-style compasses, they frequently carry a small "gumball machine" compass as an emergency backup. Even a simple "zipper pull" compass can provide accurate directions if you know how to use it. Here's the recommended procedure:

1. Squarely face the objective whose bearing you wish to determine, then frame the compass between your thumbs and forefingers, as illustrated in figure 3-7. Your index fingers form a triangle, the apex of which points to the objective.

2. Rotate the compass between your fingers until the north end of the magnetic needle points to north on the dial.

3. Hold everything rock-steady and read your bearing at the point where your forefingers touch. You should be within 5 degrees of a transit.

Now that you've mastered the workings of map and compass, you're ready to use them together as a complete navigational system. The next chapter shows you how.

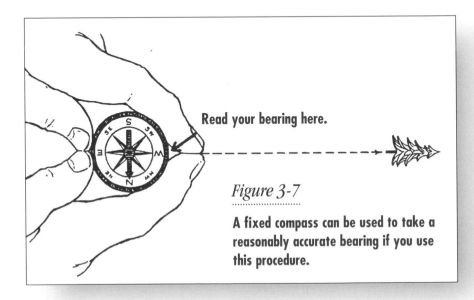

Read your bearing here.

Figure 3-7

A fixed compass can be used to take a reasonably accurate bearing if you use this procedure.

Navigation Basics

First, Some Compass Basics

The compass is graduated in degrees. There are 360 degrees in the compass circle, or *rose* (figure 4-1). The cardinal directions (north, south, east, and west) are each 90 degrees apart. Memorize the eight principal points of the compass and their relationship to the map. This will help eliminate the most common of compass errors—the 180-degree error.

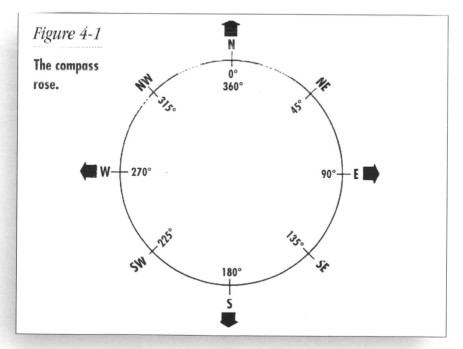

Figure 4-1

The compass rose.

For example: Assume you are fishing Lost Lake (figure 4-2) and are anchored at the peninsula at point E. You want to go to Mud Island, which lies 1½ miles to the east. With your orienteering compass you inadvertently compute a bearing of 270 degrees, which is 180 degrees in error. However, if you had mentally superimposed the compass rose over point E *before* you determined the map bearing to the island, you'd have instantly discovered your mistake.

It is not uncommon to transfer data from map to compass and make serious directional mistakes. *A knowledge of your approximate direction of travel should be known before you get down to specifics!*

Using the Compass to Determine a Map Bearing

A *bearing* is one of the 360 degree directions of the compass rose. It is always measured *clockwise* from north (either true, grid, or magnetic) to the place you want to go (your objective). For now, we'll forget about the differences between the "three norths" and simply reference our bearing to true north, that is at the top of the Lost Lake map in figure 4-2.

Assume you plan to fish the south end of Long Island, on Lost Lake. That's where the big ones are, or so you've heard! Getting to Long Island from your location at A should be easy: Just head north up the east shoreline, counting bays as you go. When you see Mud Island, hang a left around the north edge and you'll run right into your treasure spot. Easy as pie.

Don't you believe it! Look at the map scale. It's more than 12 miles to Long Island. Even on a clear day, it's doubtful you'll be able to see the intermediate islands or bays along the way. Islands and shoreline will blend to oneness. Because of wind and waves you'll lose all sense of distance traveled. You can easily mistake one of the closer islands for Mud Island, or you can get turned around completely and become convinced that a channel between islands is a large bay, or vice versa.

But getting to Long Island is easy if you have a systematic plan and a compass. The important thing, is to keep track of where you are *all the time*—easy enough if you compute bearings to intermediate check points along the way and reaffirm your position at each point. Here's the procedure:

First, pick a check point on the map. It should be some place that's reasonably close and easily identifiable—a small island, the tip of a peninsula, a prominent bay, etc. You may or may not be able to see these check points (or *attack points,* as they're called in orienteering terms) from your location at A.

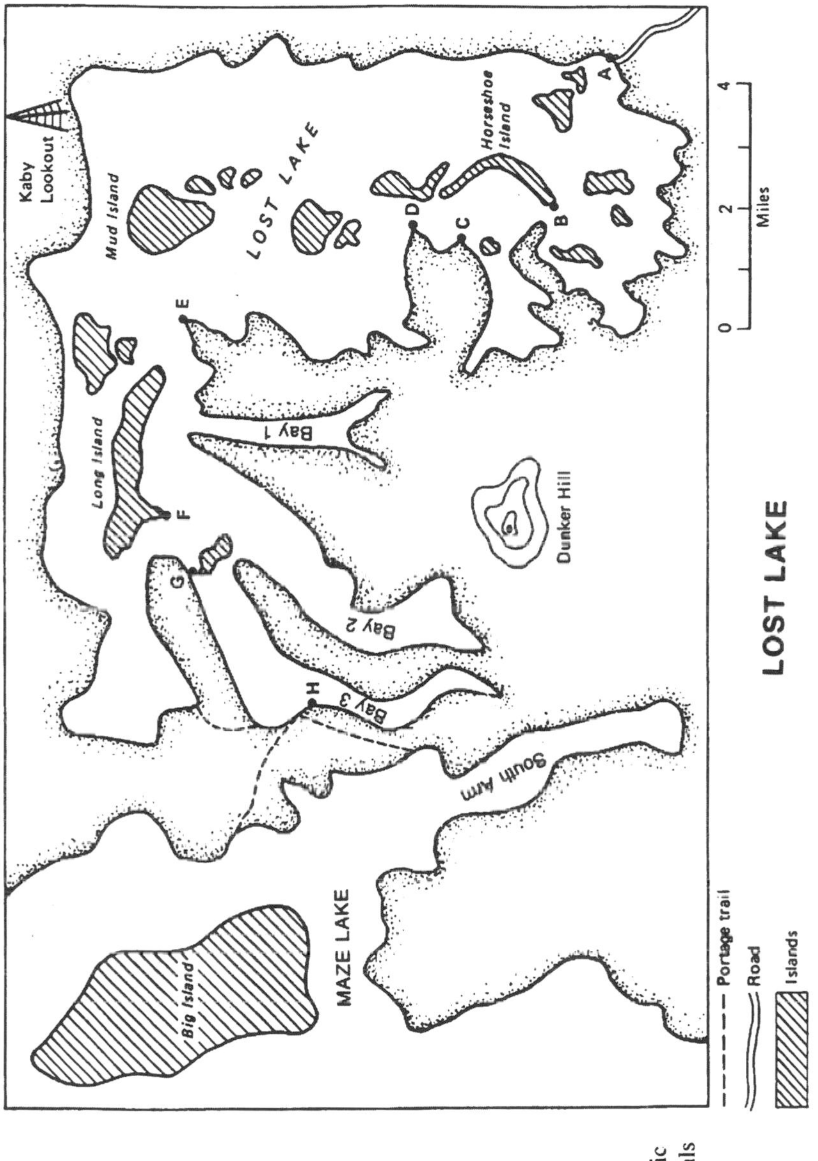
Kaby Lookout
Mud Island
LOST LAKE
Horseshoe Island
Long Island
Bay 1
Bay 2
Bay 3
South Arm
Dunker Hill
Big Island
MAZE LAKE
LOST LAKE
A
B
C
D
E
F
G
H
0
2
4
Miles
Portage trail
Road
Islands

Figure 4-2

Lost Lake Practice Map.

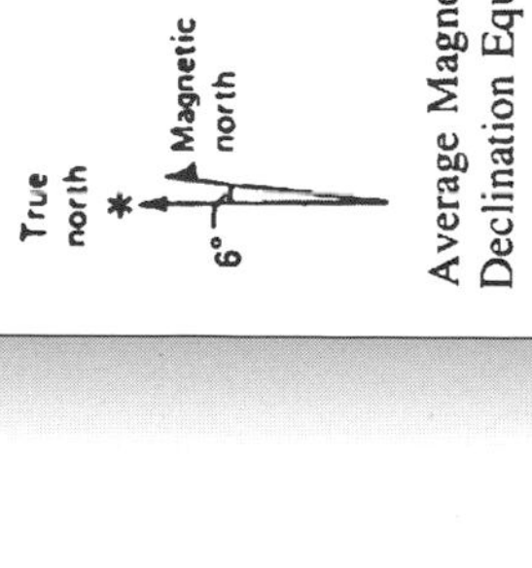
True north
Magnetic north
6°
Average Magnetic Declination Equals 6 East.

You decide that your first attack point will be the southern tip of Horseshoe Island, 2¾ miles away. Begin by guesstimating the bearing from your location at A to your objective at B. You'll be heading *northwest*, or about 315 degrees. Remember that number!

Next, determine the actual compass bearing from A to B, with your orienteering compass (preferred) or a protractor.

Protractor Method

Use this if you *don't* have an orienteering compass.

1. Draw a line from A to B.

2. Center your protractor over A and align "protractor north" with true north on your map (figure 4-3). Remember, true north is at the *top* of your map. Its direction is indicated by the starred leg of the declination diagram (more on this later) in the right map margin.

3. Read the protractor at the line intersect. You get 290 degrees.

4. Compare this figure (290 degrees) with your guesstimate of 315 degrees. Are the two within 90 degrees of one another? Good. You haven't made an error: You *know* you're going in the right direction!

Computing the Bearing with an Orienteering Compass

1. Place either the left or right edge of the compass base plate over point A. Place the forward edge of the *same* side of the base plate on point B. Your compass is now pointing in the direction you want to go—*from A to B, not from B to A* (figure 4-4).

2. *While holding the base plate tightly in position,* turn the compass housing until north on the dial points to the top (true north) of the map. *Caution:* Don't use the magnetic needle! Your direction of travel—290 degrees—is now locked onto the dial and can be read at the index inscribed on the compass base.

3. Now . . . while holding the compass in front of you with the direction-of-travel arrow inscribed on the base pointing away from your body, rotate your body with the compass until the magnetic needle points to north on the dial. Look straight ahead. You are now facing 290 degrees—toward Horseshoe Island.

4. All that's necessary now is to locate a notch or visible incongruity on the horizon that you can identify as being on this course of travel. Put your compass away, fire up your motor, and cruise towards your objective.

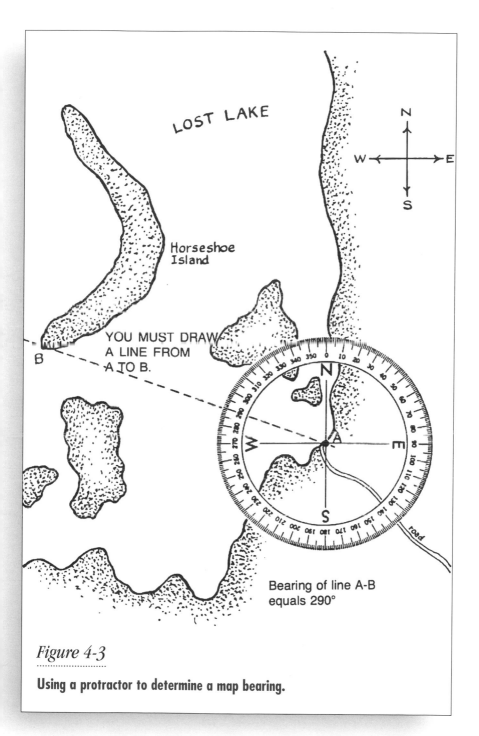

LOST LAKE

Horseshoe
Island

YOU MUST DRAW
A LINE FROM
A TO B.

B

Bearing of line A-B
equals 290°

Figure 4-3

Using a protractor to determine a map bearing.

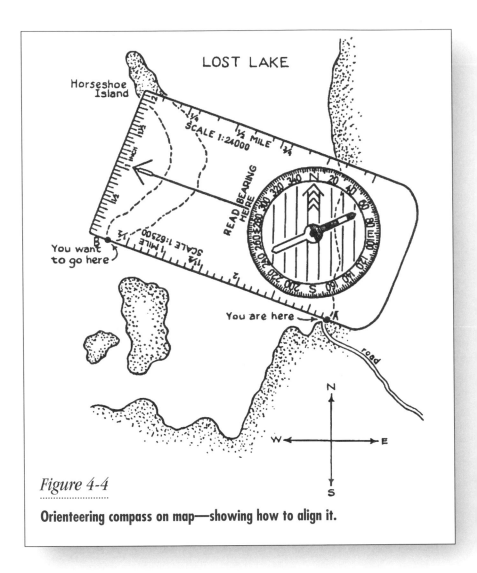

Figure 4-4

Orienteering compass on map—showing how to align it.

Note: **This is identical to the waist-high sighting method described on page 33, except that instead of shooting a bearing to a distant point, you're computing it from a map.**

Okay, test time. Use your orienteering compass or protractor to compute the true bearings from points A through G on the Lost Lake map. Check your answers below. Don't try to compute distance, travel time, or magnetic bearing. We'll get to these later.

Answers to Lost Lake Exercise

Point	True bearing	Distance (miles)	Approximate travel time	Magnetic bearing (to be set on your compass)
A to B	290°	2¾	1½ hours	284°
B to C	341°	1½	¾ hour	335°
C to D	15°	⅖	20 minutes	9°
D to E	338°	4	2 hours	332°
E to F	274°	3¼	1½ hours	268°
F to G	244°	1⅛	½ hour	238°
G to H	227°	2½	1¼ –1½ hours	221°

H to portage (paddle north up the shoreline to portage): Time— about 15 minutes.

Aiming Off

Proceeding from attack point to attack point is as useful on land as it is on water, with one exception: Trees! Getting around them necessarily means reestablishing your bearing after every "run in"— not impossible, but awkward enough to preclude pinpoint targeting of your objective. For this reason, precise compass bearings are usually modified by *aiming off.* This simple procedure ensures you'll hit your objective head-on. Consider the following scenario.

You've parked your car at point A in figure 4-5 and have hiked the trail to McClaren Lake (point B). You may take any one of the three routes on the return leg. You can hike the trail back to A—a weaving, time-consuming route, though one on which you can't possibly get confused. You can follow the trail to its end at Goldbar Lake (C), then continue on down the creek to the road at D and from here, walk 1½ miles east to your car.

But wait! Look at the topography between C and D. The value of each contour line, in feet, is labeled and circled on the map, and the contour interval, as given in the map legend, is 50 feet. Arrows mark where each contour crosses the creek. As you can see, the creek drops 300 feet (1,000 minus 700) in the 1½-mile distance from Goldbar Lake to the road, and likely, it's all through a tangle of head-high brush. Working your way down this steep slope, climbing over

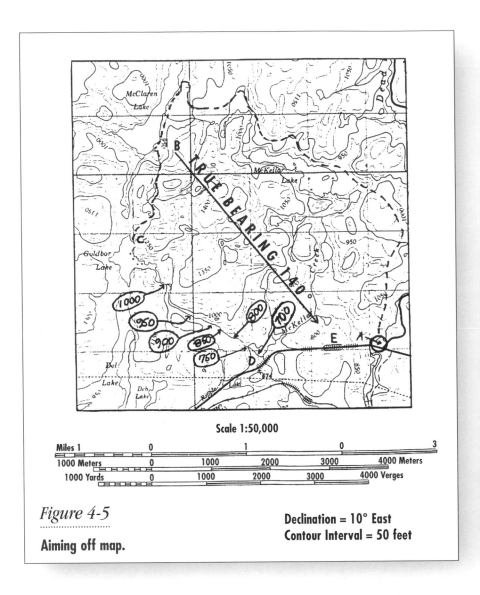

Scale 1:50,000

Figure 4-5

Aiming off map.

Declination = 10° East
Contour Interval = 50 feet

downed trees and tag alder, might take much longer—and be far more unpleasant—than backtracking over the trail.

There's an alternative, however—a straight compass shot from B to A. You'll be going overland, so it'll be tough sledding. And you'll have to avoid the scattered ponds and wade a few creeks. But it will spell adventure—the reason why you came here in the first place. And it would be awesomely remote. If you use your compass, you won't get lost.

BASIC ESSENTIALS

Let's do it! Here's the procedure.

If you compute a direct bearing from your present location at B, to A, your chance of arriving on target at the road junction is very small. After all, you'll be climbing up and down hills, skirting ponds and brush piles. That you won't be able to maintain a precise course over this rough ground is a forgone fact. Better to compensate for this error by aiming off a bit to the west—say to point E. Granted, you'll probably miss E, but you *will* strike the road somewhere east or west of it. Once you hit the road just follow it east to your starting point. Simple, isn't it?

If aiming off is useful on land, it's even more useful on water. For example: Suppose you're located at point G on the Lost Lake map (figure 4-2). You want to take the portage trail that leads to the South Arm of Maze Lake, just north of H. There are three portages leading out of Bay 3, but only one goes to South Arm. From G to the South Arm trail is about 3 miles. A 4-degree error over this distance would cause you to miss your objective by at least 1,100 feet (remember, 1 degree of compass error equals 92 feet per mile of ground error), or nearly a quarter mile—enough to send you scurrying down the wrong trail.

The solution is to aim off to H—an unidentifiable point just south of the trail. Then, when you reach the shoreline, turn right (north). The first path you come to is the right one.

Declination

A compass points (actually, it doesn't point—it lines up with the earth's magnetic field) to *magnetic* north, not *true* north. This angular difference, called *declination*, must be considered whenever you use your compass (figures 4-6, 4-7). In the eastern United States the declination is westerly; in the western United States it's easterly. If you live right on the imaginary line that goes directly through both the true and magnetic north poles (called the *agonic* line), your declination will be zero.

On the other hand, if you live east or west of the agonic line, your compass will be in error, since the true north pole is not in the same place as the magnetic north pole. As you can see from the declination chart, the farther away you are from the agonic line, the greater the declination. Moreover, the magnetic pole is constantly moving; because of this, declination will vary from year to year as well as place to place. Consequently, it's not possible for compass makers to factory-adjust a compass to account for this variation.

To find the exact declination for your area, consult your

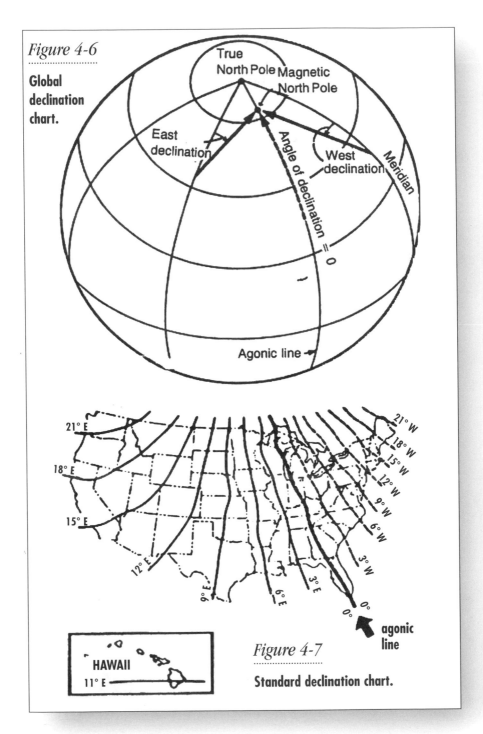

Figure 4-6

Global declination chart.

True North Pole

Magnetic North Pole

East declination

West declination

Meridian

Angle of declination = 0

Agonic line

21° E

18° E

15° E

12° E

9° E

6° E

3° E

21° W

18° W

15° W

12° W

9° W

6° W

3° W

0°

0°

agonic line

HAWAII

11° E

Figure 4-7

Standard declination chart.

topographic map. You'll find the declination value in a diagram in the lower map margin. It will look something like this:

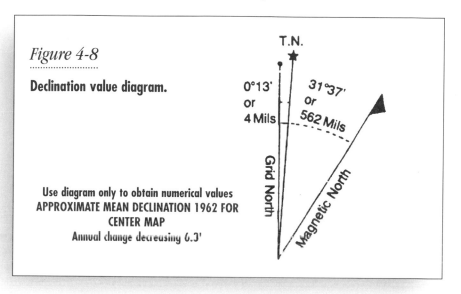

Figure 4-8

Declination value diagram.

T.N.

0°13' or 4 Mils

31°37' or 562 Mils

Grid North

Magnetic North

Use diagram only to obtain numerical values
APPROXIMATE MEAN DECLINATION 1962 FOR CENTER MAP
Annual change decreasing 6.3'

Note that the "legs" of the declination diagram in figure 4-8 *are not* drawn to angular scale (some diagrams *are*). The angles are slightly exaggerated for clarity—a note to that effect appears in the legend. Consequently, you shouldn't use the direction of the magnetic flag as an accurate pointing for your compass. Instead, adjust the instrument mathematically, as explained in the following section.

1. The star (★) indicates the direction of true north. This leg of the diagram runs parallel to a line of longitude.

2. The flag (▲) points to magnetic north. If the flag is to the right (east) of the north star, the area declination is east. If it's to the left of the star, the declination is west.

3. The black sphere (●) indicates the direction of the grid lines on the map. *Remember:* Topographic maps do not have lines of longitude imprinted on their faces, but they do have grid lines. The two *are not* the same! When you peel the skin off a globe (earth) and lay it flat, you distort the curved meridians. This distortion—or variation from true north—is reported in all declination diagrams.

Interpreting the Diagram

In figure 4-8, grid north is 13 minutes west of true north. Disregard the 4 mil number. That's for military use.*

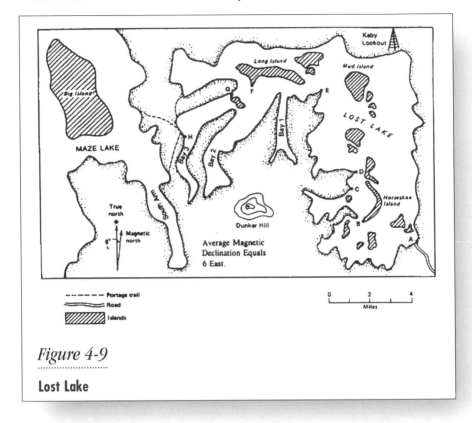

Figure 4-9

Lost Lake

Magnetic north is 31°24' (31°37'-0°13') east of true north (you should round it off to 31 degrees). This is the direction your compass needle will point. It is also the value of the *declination,* that is defined as the *angle between true north and magnetic north.*

You can also determine *grid declination* from the diagram. It is the angle between *grid north* and magnetic north—in this case, 31°37' east, or 32 degrees when rounded off. The section on grid declination on page 47 tells you how to use this important figure.

---

*The military compass is graduated in "mils." There are 6,400 mils in a circle. North is zero mils, east is 1,600 mils, south is 3,200 mils, etc. Mils are further subdivided into tenths and hundredths. Minutes and seconds are not used.

Dealing with Declination

Check out the declination on the Lost Lake map (Figure 4-9) on page 46, which is duplicated here for your convenience. It equals 6 degrees east. There are no grid lines on this map, hence, no need to identify *"grid"* north.

As stated, maps are almost always drawn in their true perspective (any variation here is so small it can be ignored). So any bearing you determine *from the map* by using the top of the map or the east or west border (line of longitude) as a north reference, is, by definition, a *true* bearing. The bearings you computed in the A-through-G "point-to-point" exercise were therefore all true bearings. *Now, you must change these true values to magnetic ones that will be set on your compass* and followed on the ground—easy enough, if you remember the simple rhyme:

Declination east—compass least
(subtract east declination from your map direction).
Declination west—compass best
(add west declination to your map direction).

Your true bearing from A to B in the Lost Lake exercise was 290 degrees. Change it to a magnetic bearing by application of the rhyme. *Subtract* six degrees and you get 284. Adjust your compass for this new heading and take off. You'll hit point B head-on.

Conversely, if the declination were west, you would add its value (290 + 6 = 296) to your compass reading.

Note: **It makes no difference in which direction (north, south, east, or west, or something in between) you are going on the map sheet. If the declination is east, you always subtract its value from your true map bearing. If it's west, you add it. If this is confusing, you may want to buy a compass that can be adjusted for declination.**

Okay, test time ... again. Convert all your *true* Lost Lake bearings to *magnetic* ones. Answers are on page 41.

Grid Declination

Grid lines take the guess work out of aligning your protractor or orienteering compass to map north. Remember, however, that *grid lines don't point true north,* so you'll have to compensate for their variation.

Any bearing you compute off a map, using *grid north* (any grid line) as the north reference line is, by definition, a *grid bearing*. Before you can follow this bearing on the ground, you must first convert it to a *magnetic bearing* by application of the "east is least, west is best" rhyme.

The grid declination in figure 4-8 is 31°37' east, or 32 degrees, when rounded off. Subtract 32 degrees from your grid bearing and set this value on your compass. That's all there is to it. The procedure is identical to that used to change a true bearing to a magnetic one.

In truth, we're splitting hairs here, for grid north is so close to true north (just 13 minutes away) that the difference is meaningless. This isn't always the case, however, so check out the values before you commit to your *accurate* field bearings. Admittedly, true and grid north seldom vary by much more than 3 degrees, so for typical field use the two can usually be considered as one.

Tape Method of Adjusting the Compass for Declination

If you don't want to mess with the mechanics of adding or subtracting declination values from your true or grid bearings, you can adjust your compass to compensate. Here's how.

Given: You have computed a *true* map bearing of 60 degrees to your objective. The area declination is 10 degrees east.

Procedure: Place a narrow piece of tape across the face of the compass housing so that it goes over the needle pivot and intersects both the 10-degree and 190-degree marks. Your compass is now adjusted to compensate for a 10-degree east declination.

Now ... hold the compass in front of you and find the bearing on the ground—only *don't* frame the magnetic needle in the doghouse (printed arrow in the capsule) as is customary. Instead, align it with the tape mark, which is 10 degrees east of north. Note that you are actually facing a bearing of 50 (60 degrees minus 10 degrees).

Conversely, if the declination were 10 degrees west, you would apply the tape so that it intersected the 350-degree (that's 10 degrees west) and 170-degree marks. As you might guess, the mechanical declination adjustments on sophisticated compasses use this very procedure.

Adjusting Your Map for Declination

You can also adjust your map for declination by drawing lines that run parallel to the north magnetic pole, across its face. Then, when you compute map headings, just align the printed arrow in the capsule of your orienteering compass with these lines, rather than "map north" (top of the map). All competitive orienteering maps are set up like this. However, the system works much better with small orienteering maps than with 2½-foot-square topos. Try drawing parallel lines across a standard-sized topographic map and you'll see why. Best stick with a more conventional treatment of declination.

Updating the Declination

The magnetic poles are constantly moving. Their location changes from year to year (and from minute to minute). Movements are subtle, however—generally small enough that only surveyors interested in extreme accuracy need worry about them.

The problem only surfaces when you're working off a very old map. For example, the legend in figure 4-8 states 'APPROXIMATE MEAN DECLINATION 1962 . . . annual change decreasing 6.3'.'

This means that magnetic north (the flag) is moving *westward* (decreasing) by 6.3 minutes per year. Updating the declination to 1989 is easy:

1. Determine the elapsed years (1999 - 1962 = 37 years).

2. Multiply the annual change by the elapsed years (6.3' x 37 years) = 233.1 minutes.

3. Convert minutes to whole degrees (233.1 ÷ 60 = 3.9 . . . or 4 degrees.

4. Subtract this figure from the 1962 declination of 31 degrees ($31°$ - $4°$ = $27°$). Your declination for 1999 is 27 degrees east.

Note: **To update the grid declination, merely subtract 4 degrees from the grid magnetic angle of 32 degrees. Answer: 28 degrees east.**

Position by Triangulation

Suppose you're lost on a large, maze-like lake, but you can recognize two or more topographical features off in the distance. Use your orienteering compass (or protractor and conventional compass) to find your position by *triangulation*.

Pick out one point on the horizon that you can identify—Old Baldy, in this case (see figure 4-10). Shoot a magnetic bearing to the point (bearing = 312 degrees). Change this magnetic bearing to a true

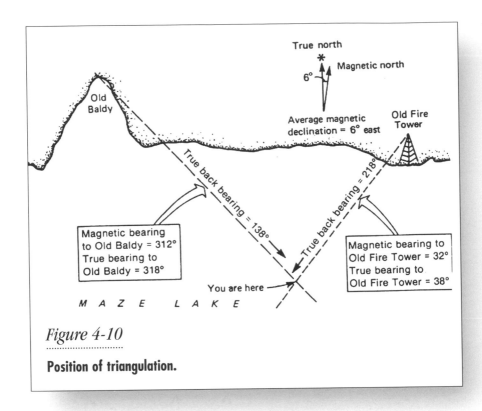

True north

Magnetic north

6°

Average magnetic declination = 6° east

Old Baldy

Old Fire Tower

True back bearing = 138°

True back bearing = 218°

Magnetic bearing
to Old Baldy = 312°
True bearing to
Old Baldy = 318°

Magnetic bearing to
Old Fire Tower = 32°
True bearing to
Old Fire Tower = 38°

You are here

M A Z E   L A K E

Figure 4-10

Position of triangulation.

bearing by reverse application of the rhyme: 312° + 6° = 318°. Draw the back (reciprocal) bearing (318° – 180° = 138°) through Old Baldy, using your compass base plate and a sharp pencil.

> *Tip:* **When using an orienteering compass you don't have to compute the back bearing at all. Simply set 318 degrees on the compass dial, place your pencil point on Old Baldy, and put the forward edge of one side of the base plate against the pencil point. Rotate the entire compass in an arc about the pencil until north on the dial (not the needle) points to the top (true north) of the map.** *Caution:* **Do not turn the compass housing during this operation, since the true bearing that you just computed to Old Baldy (318°) is set on the dial. This procedure will not work if you change the dial setting!**

Now . . . using the base plate as a straight edge, draw your line. Repeat the exercise using another point that you can identify (the old fire tower). You are located where the two lines cross.

Okay, now for another test, using the Lost Lake map. You can identify

Dunker Hill at a magnetic bearing of 253 degrees and Kaby Lookout at a magnetic bearing of 4 degrees. Where are you located? *Clue:* Don't forget to apply the declination. You'll find the answer on page 52.

Relocating a Good Fishing Spot by Triangulation

You don't need to identify points on a map to use triangulation. In fact, you don't need a map at all! Suppose you've discovered a real hot spot—the fish are biting like crazy. You definitely want to come here again! Problem is, there are no identifying landmarks to guide the way. And the fishing hole is small, just a dozen yards in diameter. How on earth will you find this place again?

Easy! Just shoot compass bearings to two or more places on the shoreline. The tall pine on the right (figure 4-11) and broken-down cabin at left are ideal. But your points need not be so sophisticated. A moss-covered boulder or leaning tree will do. Anything that won't "run off" will work. Since you don't have a map, there's no need to compute back bearings, or to draw intersecting lines. Instead, simply record the numbers in a notebook for future reference. Next time you come here, look for the cabin and pine tree. Then, position yourself where the two bearings match.

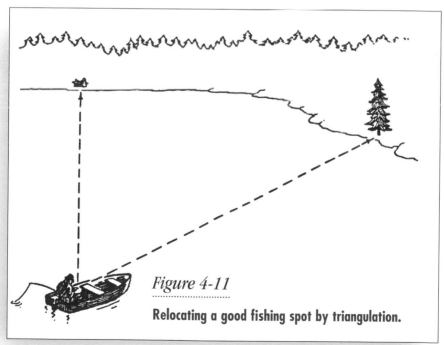

Figure 4-11

Relocating a good fishing spot by triangulation.

Free Triangulation

This is the same as two-point triangulation, except you need just one reference line. Assume you're hiking along the railroad track in figure 4-12 and want to establish your exact position. In the distance you see a large hill that stands out boldly among the flatlands. You shoot a compass bearing to the hill and get 156 degrees.

Convert this *magnetic* reading to *true* direction by reverse application of the rhyme: 156° + 10° = 166°. Next, determine the *back bearing* (166° + 180° = 346°) and plot it on the map. You're located where the line crosses the track.

Use free triangulation any place you can establish a single line of reference—a road, trail, river, creek, lakeshore, or power line.

Answer to triangulation problem: You are located at the north end of Horseshoe Island.

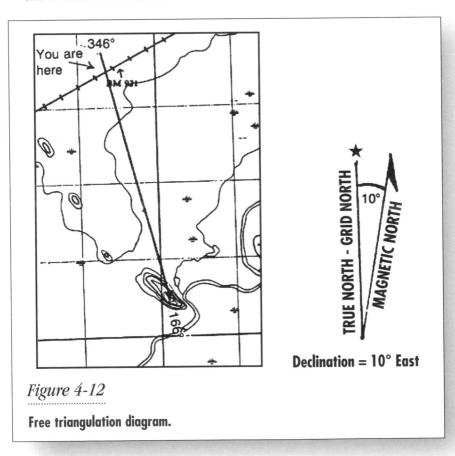

Declination = 10° East

Figure 4-12

Free triangulation diagram.

Tricks of the Trade

If you've progressed this far, you're just short of being expert with map and compass. You can now compute map bearings, convert them to magnetic readings, and chart a course through tangled brush or the maze of islands on a fog-bound lake. You know all about aiming off, triangulation, and declination plus a wealth of other navigation procedures.

So congratulations on your hard-earned confidence. You're almost ready to cope with the worst of times on the best of terms. What you need now is practice, practice, practice . . . plus a working knowledge of some tricks of the trade. Here are a few.

Navigation at Night

Over the years I've done a fair amount of black night canoe travel on large sprawling lakes. Most memorable was the time I camped in the Boundary Waters Canoe Area of Minnesota and was awakened to find three bears merrily munching dehydrated prunes that my teen group had carelessly thrown about. We blew whistles, clanged pans, and yelled loudly. No luck. The bruins remained oblivious to the racket and kept right on eating.

When they knocked down one tent, we decided it was time to leave. Within minutes we struck camp and put to sea. There was no moon or stars; just full cloud cover and vast nothingness. Visibility was a flat zero.

Fortunately, I had a flashlight and my Silva Ranger compass. I carefully plotted a beeline for a distant island that had a campsite. Then I set the compass on the floor of my canoe and unerringly kept the luminous point on the magnetic needle aligned with the glowing aid dots that flanked it.

Before we dipped paddles, I carefully computed the distance from our location to the island. It was almost exactly 3 miles. At an approximate paddling speed of 2 cautious miles per hour, we should arrive on target in ninety minutes. I set my watch alarm and peeled out into the blackness of the night.

Exactly eighty minutes later, we touched shore. There was the island . . . and the welcome campsite.

Moral: You need more than good bearings for black night travel. You also need to keep track of your distance and time!

Problem: **Calculate the distance between points on the Lost Lake practice map in chapter 4. Assume a travel speed of 2 miles per hour. Check your answers on page 41.**

Traveling overland on a dead dark night is another matter. Some years ago, as a forester with the Bureau of Land Management in Oregon, I was lost for three days in the mountains south of Coos Bay. Again, I had my trusty Silva, but this time, no map. Referencing was a "matter of the mind": I knew Highway 101 was about 60 miles due west. I tried to travel the first night, but it was no use. After a number of life-threatening falls, I gave up in disgust and waited till sunrise.

Around noon of the third day, I struck a logging road and the sound of a clanging diesel tractor. Humility? You bet. When I returned to work the next day, I never told a soul. After all . . . foresters don't get lost!

Outdoor books are rich with tales of men who traveled the haunting wilds with only the stars or a simple compass to guide them. Of course, it *can* be done and has been done, but the risks of injury are very real.

However, night travel takes on new dimensions if the sky is gentle gray or if you have a full moon or powerful headlamp to guide the way. And oh yes, don't rely on luminous compass points to keep you on track. Compass "night sights" are very primitive: Without frequent light to recharge their chemical batteries, they fail. None will last the night. A flashlight—or other light source—is essential.

As to navigation by the stars (discounting *celestial* navigation, of course), I know of no one who has ever had to resort to such folly. If you are lost or without a compass, you have no business traveling at night, and if you do have a compass you certainly don't need the stars. Moreover, trees and topographical features sometimes prevent you from keeping the North Star in view. Such star navigation makes interesting reading, but it's impractical. However, if you're interested in this sort of thing, check out a Boy Scout handbook or standard text on surveying.

River Navigation

Everything in this book has been necessarily centered around land and lake navigation. After all, that's where you'll be navigating most of the time. But suppose you want to canoe or raft a wild, brawny river. Are there navigational concerns other than those mentioned in chapter 2?

You bet! With the impact of man on river systems, it is becoming more and more important for river users to know what the water conditions are before they go afloat. Many local and even far northern rivers are now dam-controlled and are very dangerous at high water or impossible during the "walking levels" of late summer. Barbed-wire fences strung across rivers maim and kill boaters each year, and the people who string these fences usually have the law on their side. Each year, we read about canoeists and fishermen who inadvertently paddled over a dam because they didn't know it was there.

If you boat rivers, you must be able to accurately locate and identify dams, rapids, fences, and other obstacles that can endanger your trip. The symbols for many of these appear on your topographic map, but not all. And frequently what's there is incorrect. Here are some ways to outfox the inadequacies of your map.

1. Continually check the *level* of the tree line as you paddle along. If tree heights fall off suddenly, there's a dam or falls ahead.

2. Maps do not indicate obstacles that are the result of river turbulence. Waves pile up on the *outside* of bends, and so does debris. Except in very low water, you should always stay on the *inside* curves of a river.

3. It is very difficult to fix your position on a river. A compass will be useful for rough directions only. Of course, you can reaffirm your location at major bends, rapids, or incoming streams, or you may be fortunate enough to locate an identifiable object upon which you can plot a line of free triangulation.

Lastly, some of the best sources of river conditions are the people who live in the area. Always check with them before embarking on a river, even if you've run it many times. Be aware, however, that locals tend to exaggerate the dangers of their river. So especially seek out foresters or professional people who work in the area. Outdoors people will generally tell it like it is . . . or at least they'll exaggerate less.

And if one day your dreams take you to the far north, where rivers run cold and help is an airplane ride away, you'll need to know (*absolutely know!*) your precise location at all times. Contrary to what you may have read or heard, compasses are generally quite reliable near the Arctic Circle—that is, if you can correctly apply the declination—which may change with each few miles you travel!

Navigating Streams and Moose Trails

Finding your way through a maze of beaver streams and moose trails calls for resourcefulness. Remember, modern maps are made from aerial photos, and if you can't see the sky because of a dense tree canopy or tall grass, the plane-mounted camera can't see the stream. Therefore, your map may be in error in these places, though the general flow of the water course—minus the switchbacks—is usually accurate.

The heads and mouths of small streams are almost always plotted correctly, but deciphering the maze in between often calls for a ready compass. Moreover, stream beds are constantly changing, and these changes will not be reflected on a topographic map that is many years old.

Some hints for navigating small meandering streams: 1) Where a stream forks, take the route with the strongest flow, even if it looks more restrictive than a broader channel. If there is no discernible current, note which way the grass bends in the channel and follow; 2) Check your compass frequently— don't rely on your map, especially if it is many years old; 3) If you come to a dead end and see a portage trail, scout it before you carry your canoe or boat across. Your "portage" may simply be a heavily used animal trail that leads to a connecting tributary or a dead-end pond.

Your Watch as a Compass

Although of questionable accuracy, direction finding using a watch is at times convenient when you want a rough, quick direction but you don't want to get out your compass. If your watch is correctly set for the time zone in which you're traveling, just hold the watch horizontal and point the hour hand at the sun. Half-way between the hour hand and twelve o'clock is south. Such showmanship will impress your friends when things get dull on a long trip

By the way, you can also use your compass as a watch (see figure 5-1). Just keep in mind the hourly positions of the sun, which are

6:00 A.M.—*east*	3:00 P.M.—*southwest*
9:00 A.M.—*southeast*	6:00 P.M.—*west*
NOON—*south*	

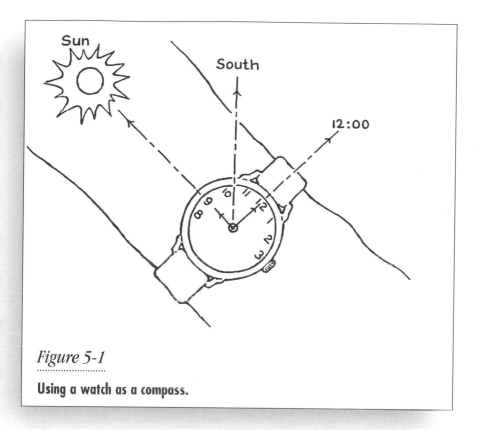

Figure 5-1

Using a watch as a compass.

Using the Stars as a Compass

Follow the two "pointer" stars on the cup of the Big Dipper to the North Star (Polaris), which is the tail star of the Little Dipper (figure 5-2). The Dippers are "circumpolar" constellations, so they're visible all year round from any place in the Northern Hemisphere. Polaris is seldom more than one degree east or west of true north.

To Determine Declination by the Stars

If your map does not provide magnetic declination information, drive two pointed sticks into the ground and line them up with the North Star, as illustrated in figure 5-3. The longer stick should be "north" of the shorter stick. The angle between the compass needle and true north is the magnetic declination of your area. Be sure to note whether the declination is east or west! Naturally, this procedure works best when declination angles are very large.

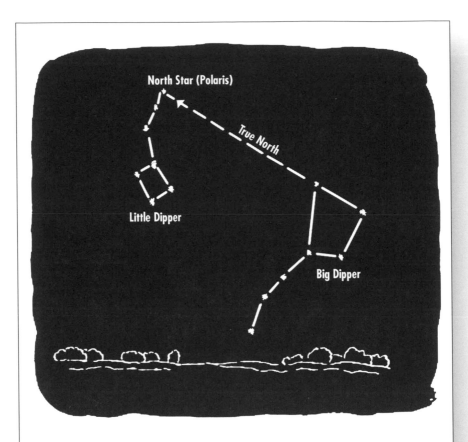

Figure 5-2

How to tell north by using the stars.

The Global Positioning System (GPS)

GPS (global positioning system) receivers are hot new navigational aids. Twenty-four satellites that orbit Earth twice a day transmit precise time (via an atomic clock) and positioning information. With a GPS receiver you can determine your location on Earth to within 100 meters or less in a matter of minutes or seconds. Or you can enter a set of coordinates of a place you want to go, and the GPS receiver will provide a compass bearing and distance that will be updated by satellite information as you walk, drive, fly, or paddle. Press a button and you get a speed readout and an estimated time of arrival (ETA).

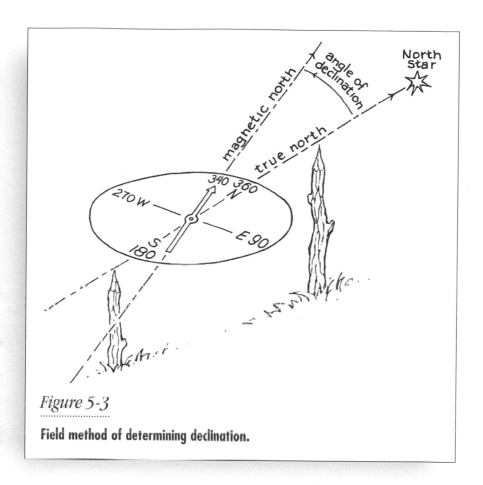

Figure 5-3

Field method of determining declination.

Even without a map, a GPS is extremely useful. Enter your starting position and save it as a way point. Establish other way points as you proceed—then, like Hansel and Gretel, follow your electronic bread crumbs home.

When the military discovered that GPS receivers were accurate to within 25 meters, rather than the anticipated 100 meters, they became concerned that an enemy might use GPS to target a missile. They consequently introduced into the civilian GPS signal what is called Selective Availability (SA)—a random error that varies from 25 to 100 meters. However, my own experience with a Magellan Trailblazer GPS suggests that most of the error is in the elevation mode. I've used my Magellan for two summers in the Canadian Arctic and have found that fixes seldom err by more than 25 meters.

Most of today's GPS receivers are "menu driven," which somewhat simplifies operation. Nonetheless, mastery of the instrument requires considerable study plus a working knowledge of maps and navigational procedures. All hand-held GPS units operate on small batteries, which could fail when you need them most. For this reason, it's impractical to leave the instrument on for continuous positioning. The most useful GPS feature is its ability to verify your location on a map. Also be aware that most inexpensive civilian GPS models are *water-repellent,* not waterproof, so you don't dare use them in heavy rain.

Maps must have some sort of reference system to which your GPS can relate. United States and Canadian topographic maps are marked with degrees of latitude and longitude. Canadian topographic maps and U.S. military maps also use the Universal Trans Mercator (UTM) system that is simpler because it's decimal-oriented. Any GPS can be set to read Lat/Lon or UTM coordinates, as you prefer. Some maps, which are made by private companies for use in specialized areas such as national parks and wilderness areas, don't have either UTM or Lat/Lon markings, which means you can't use your GPS with them.

A GPS receiver will not replace your map and compass, but it will add to the fun—and safety—of exploring wild places.

Baselines

Most every book on wilderness navigation has a chapter devoted to "the lost hunter"—relocating your remote camp, finding the remains of the deer you shot, etc. But it's all simply a matter of baselines, that is, you establish a reliable handrail (road, stream, powerline, etc.) Then use it as a reference line for your bearings. Figure 1-1 is a typical example of this relationship—one which again proves the importance of a map. Note, however, that you don't need a formal map to travel the backwoods with confidence. A mind relationship is often enough. My three-day "confusion" in the Oregon woods is a case in point. I knew Highway 101 was due west. And that was sufficient!

As you can see, there's no substitute for common sense. To this add a good map and a compass and a practiced hand, and you'll have all the tools you need to confidently navigate the backcountry.

Appendix 1
Common U.S. Map Symbols

Topographic Map Symbols

Primary highway		Gravel beach or glacial moraine	
Secondary highway		Woods (green)	
Light-duty road		Scrub (green)	
Unimproved road		Orchard (green)	
Trail		Rock bare or awash	
Bridge		Group of rocks bare or awash	
Building: small; large		Sunken rock	
Cemetery: small; large		Intermittent stream	
Standard gauge single track; station		Disappearing stream	
Abandoned track		Large falls; large rapids	
Power transmission line; pole; tower		Masonry dam	
Telephone or telegraph line		Intermittent lake or pond	
Quarry or open pit mine		Dry lake	
Mine tunnel or cave entrance		Water well; spring or seep	
Sand or mud area, dunes or shifting sand		Marsh or swamp	

Appendix 2
Common Terms

Agonic line: A line or zero declination. At any point along this imaginary line, the compass will point true north.

Aiming off: The navigator aims to the right or left of his objective, rather than straight at it. This creates a purposeful error in a known direction, which helps in targeting the objective. See pages 41-43 for details.

Attack point: A point on the map that is easy to identify on land (hilltop, road junction, railroad crossing, etc.). Same as a "check point."

Back bearing: Also called reciprocal bearing. It is the opposite direction from which you came. Or 180 degrees plus or minus your forward bearing.

Baseline: A handrail that's used as a reference line for positioning when afield. The navigator works on one side or the other of the baseline. A return bearing is plotted to the baseline, which is then followed "home."

Base plate: The ruled plastic base of an orienteering compass.

Bearing: A direction, in degrees, from where you are to where you want to go. Technically, it's a horizontal angle measured from north to your direction of travel.

Cardinal points: The primary directions—north, east, south, west.

Compasses: See index for compass types and their differences.

Compass rose: The 360 degrees of the compass circle.

Contour interval: The difference in elevation (usually above sea level) from one contour line to another.

Contour lines: Light brown lines on a map that indicate height above sea level.

Declination: The direction in which the compass needle points. More accurately, it's the angular difference between true north and magnetic north, or between grid north and magnetic north (called "grid declination"). Expressed in degrees east or west of the agonic line.

Declination diagram: A diagram in the legend of topographic maps that gives the value of the area declination.

Doghouse: A slang term for the printed arrow inside the housing of orienteering compasses. When the "dog" is in the "house" (magnetic needle inside printed arrow of housing), the compass is properly oriented.

Direction-of-travel arrow: An arrow inscribed on the plastic base plate of orienteering compasses points towards your objective when the compass is properly oriented (needle centered in the doghouse).

GPS (global positioning system): An electronic unit that receives positioning information off orbiting satellites. With a civilian model GPS, you can locate your position anywhere on Earth in a matter of minutes. Accuracy is 100 meters or less.

Grid lines: Interconnecting lines superimposed over the face of topographic maps.

Grid north: The direction the grid lines point with respect to true north.

Handrail: A topographic feature that you can follow to your objective, such as a road, river, creek, power line, trail, or lakeshore.

Housing: The part of the compass which contains the magnetic needle.

Index: A master map that contains information for ordering topographical maps. Also the place on a compass where the bearing is read.

Intercardinal points: Intermediate compass points—northeast, southeast, southwest, northwest.

Latitude: The distance in degrees north or south of the equator.

Longitude: The distance in degrees east or west of the prime meridian located at Greenwich, England.

Magnetic north: The direction the compass needle points.

Map aid lines: Parallel lines inside the housing of orienteering compasses. When these are aligned to map north, the compass will give a proper bearing you can follow on the ground.

Meridians: Same as lines of longitude. Meridians run true north and south.

NCIC (National Cartographic Information Service): The federal clearinghouse for special purpose maps and cartographic information.

North: There are three norths—true (geographic), magnetic (direction the compass needle points), and grid (direction the grid lines run).

Orienteering: Competitive sport combining cross-country running and compass directions to locate specific points (called controls) on the ground.

Parallels: Lines of latitude. These run "parallel" to the equator.

Planimetric map: A map that does not indicate elevation above sea level. Example, a common road map.

Protractor: A plastic arc used for measuring angles.

Scale: The relationship between map and ground distance. Expressed as a representative fraction, such as 1:250,000.

Symbols: Icons on maps that depict primarily man-made features.

Topographic map: A map that shows topography in three dimensions with the aid of contour lines.

USGS (United States Geological Survey): Place where you order topographic maps.

Variation: A nautical term for declination.

Index

About the Author

Cliff Jacobson is one of North America's most respected outdoors writers and wilderness guides. He is a professional canoe outfitter and guide for the Science Museum of Minnesota and a wilderness canoeing consultant for Eckerd Family Youth Alternatives, Inc. When he's not canoeing, Cliff also teaches eighth grade environmental science as well as Wilderness Experience, a program he developed for students at risk. He is strongly committed to the ethics of "leave no trace" camping.

Cliff has authored sixteen outdoors books and numerous educational publications, including Canoeing Wild Rivers, considered by many to be one of the most authoritative resources of its kind. Three of his titles were among the top ten best-selling outdoors books in 1996. He has also written for the Minnesota Department of Natural Resources, and he developed the orienteering materials for Minnesota Schools. His water-quality program, Water Water Everywhere, written for the Hach Co,. is widely used in schools, and his Wilderness Meal program is an extremely popular environmental education activity.